easy crochet
Flowers

easy crochet
Flowers

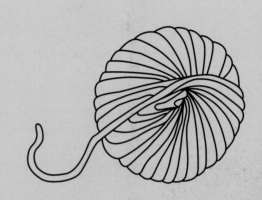

30 projects to make for your home and to wear

Consultant: Nikki Trench

hamlyn

An Hachette UK Company
www.hachette.co.uk

First published in Great Britain in 2013 by
Hamlyn, a division of Octopus Publishing Group Ltd
Endeavour House
189 Shaftesbury Avenue
London
WC2H 8JY
www.octopusbooks.co.uk

ISBN 978-0-600-62836-1

A CIP catalogue record for this book is available from the
British Library

Printed and bound in China

10 9 8 7 6 5 4 3 2 1

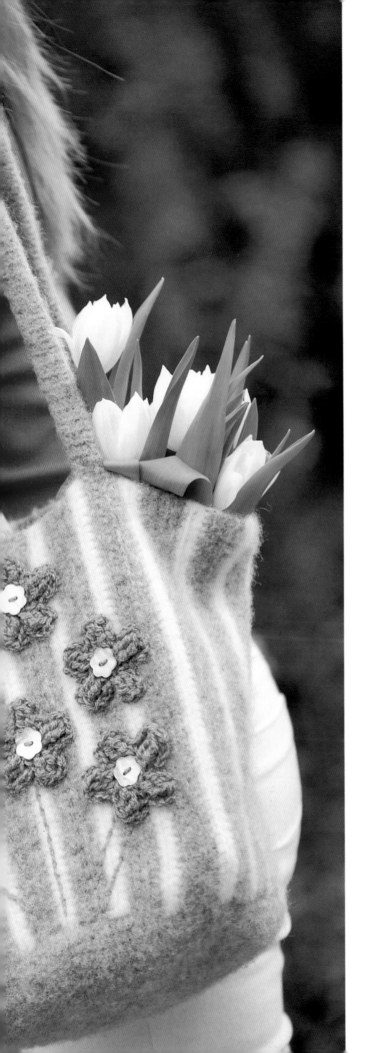

Contents

Introduction 6

Flower head cuff 8

Folk-art cushion 12

Hippy belt 16

Mini corsages 20

Floral medallion scarf 24

Trio of bracelets 28

Flower corsage tote bag 32

Flower scarf 36

Flower-edged jacket 40

Floral napkin rings 44

Felted bag with flower motifs 48

Trilby hatbands 52

Bolero with flower motifs 56

Embossed scarf 60

Floral hairband 64

Funky flower mats 68

Floral appliqué vest 72

Rose cushion 76

Flower-trimmed mesh gloves 80

Flower-sprinkled bag 84

Garden kneeler 88

Beads and flowers hair clip 92

Heart-shaped purse 96

Spring fever scarf 100

Flower band hat 104

Funky tea cosy 108

Clutch bag with flowers 112

Cupcake pincushions 116

Daisy-edged bolero 120

Flower-trimmed clutch bag 124

Index 128

Introduction

Crochet is easy, and it grows fast. Master a few basic stitches (and the terminology) and you can create stylish crocheted items to wear, use to decorate your home and as gifts for friends and family in next to no time and with minimal experience.

Whether you are a relative beginner, a confident convert or a long-term aficionado, there are projects here to delight. While your first attempts may be a bit uneven, a little practice and experimentation will ensure you soon improve. None of the projects in this book is beyond the scope of even those fairly new to the hobby. Even the most basic of stitches can be translated into covetable items.

Flowers, enduringly popular with crafters, are ideal to crochet, and they make attractive adornments for the projects in this book, which range from stylish items you can wear – hats, belts, scarves and even jackets – through to items for the home such as cushions and table mats. All would make charming, unique gifts.

Crochet essentials

All you really need to get crocheting is a hook and some yarn. For many projects that's it, and where additional items are required, most of these can be found in a fairly basic sewing kit. All measurements are given in metric and imperial. Choose which to work in and stick with it since conversions may not be exact in all instances.

- **Hooks** These are sized in mm (with 'old UK' sizes given as well) and can be made from wood, plastic, aluminium, bamboo or steel. The material affects the weight and 'feel' of the hook, and which you choose is largely down to personal preference.
- **Yarns** Specific yarns are given for each project, but if you want to make substitutions, full details of the yarn's composition and the ball lengths are given so that you can choose alternatives, either from the wide range of online sources, or from your local supplier,

many of whom have very knowledgeable staff. Do keep any leftover yarns (not forgetting the ball bands, since these contain vital information) to use for future projects.
- **Additional items** Some of the projects require making up and finishing, and need further materials and equipment, such as needles (both ordinary and round-pointed tapestry ones) and thread, buttons, ribbons and other accessories. These are detailed for each project in the Getting Started box.

What is in this book

All projects are illustrated with several photographs to show you the detail of the work – both inspirational and useful for reference. A full summary of each project is given in the Getting Started box so you can see exactly what's involved. Here, projects are graded from one star (straightforward, suitable for beginners) through two (more challenging) to three stars (for crocheters with more confidence and experience).

Also in the Getting Started box is the size of each finished item, yarn(s) and additional materials needed, and what tension the project is worked in. Finally, a breakdown of the steps involved is given so you know exactly what the project entails before you start.

At the start of the pattern instructions is a key to all abbreviations particular to the project and occasional notes expand if necessary.

Additional information

Occasionally, more information is needed, or a slightly specialist technique is used. A How To box on page 11 shows in detail how to make a crocheted double flower, and in other projects a diagram shows exactly how to lay out the flower elements when making the items up.

If you have enjoyed the projects here, you may want to explore the other titles in the Easy Crochet series: *Babies & Children*, *Country*, *Seaside*, *Vintage & Retro* and *Weekend*. For those who enjoy knitting, a sister series Easy Knitting, features similarly stylish yet simple projects.

Flower head cuff

Channel your inner hippie with this stretchy headband.

Tune in to flower power with this head cuff that consists of a deep band of ridged trebles and a layered floral motif that's made separately and stitched on afterwards.

GETTING STARTED

 This is a good project for a beginner to practise their crochet.

Size:
To fit head 56cm (21½in) in circumference, or as required

How much yarn:
1 x 50g (1¾oz) ball of Sublime Soya Cotton DK in colour A – Pomegranate (shade 88)
Oddment of DK cotton yarn in a contrasting colour B

Hook:
3.50mm (UK 9) crochet hook

Tension:
21 sts and 10 rows measure 10cm (4in) square over patt on 3.50mm (UK 9) hook
IT IS ESSENTIAL TO WORK TO THE STATED TENSION TO ACHIEVE SUCCESS

What you have to do:
Work head cuff in rows of trebles, working into back loop only of each stitch to give a ridged effect. Work flower in rounds using two colours. Sew flower to head cuff.

The Yarn
Sublime Soya Cotton DK (approx. 110m/120 yards per 50g/1¾oz ball) contains 50% soya-sourced viscose and 50% cotton. A natural yarn, it makes a comfortable-to-wear, luxurious fabric. It is machine-washable and there is a wide colour range.

Instructions

Abbreviations:
ch = chain
cm = centimetre(s)
dc = double crochet
htr = half treble
patt = pattern
rep = repeat
sp = space
ss = slip stitch
st(s) = stitch(es)
tr = treble

HEAD CUFF:
With 3.50mm (UK 9) hook and A, make 18ch.

Foundation row: 1tr into 4th ch from hook, 1tr into each ch to end, turn. 16 sts.

1st row: 3ch (counts as first tr), miss st at base of ch, 1tr into back loop only of each st to end, working last tr into 3rd of 3ch, turn.

Rep last row to form patt until length fits snugly around head, ending with an even number of rows. Fasten off.

FLOWER:
With 3.50mm (UK 9) hook, A and leaving a tail of yarn about 25cm (10in) long, make 6ch, join with a ss into first ch to form a circle.

1st round: 1ch, working over starting tail and into ring, work 11dc, join with a ss into first ch. 12 sts.

2nd round: 3ch, (miss next st, 1dc into next st, 2ch) 5 times, join with a ss into first of 3ch.

3rd round: (1dc, 1htr, 1tr, 1htr, 1dc) into each 2ch sp all round, ss into first dc. 6 petals made. Fasten off A.

4th round: Join B to any dc of 2nd round, inserting hook from back and around stem of st, 1ch, (4ch, 1dc around next dc of 2nd round, inserting hook as before) 5 times, 4ch, join with a ss into first ch.

5th round: (1dc, 1htr, 3tr, 1htr, 1dc) into each 4ch loop, ss into first dc. Fasten off.

Making up

Join short ends of head cuff to form a circle. Pull gently on starting tail of flower to close centre neatly. Use this tail to sew flower in place to cover seam of head cuff.

HOW TO
MAKE THE FLOWER

1 Leave a tail about 25cm (10in) long with yarn A and make six chains. Join with a slip stitch into the first chain to form a circle. For the first round, make one chain and then work eleven double crochet into the ring, over the yarn tail, and join with a slip stitch into the first chain.

2 For the second round, make three chains, miss the next stitch, make one double crochet into the next stitch and two chains. Repeat this five times and join with a slip stitch into the first of the three chains.

3 For the third round, make one double crochet, one half treble, one treble, one half treble and one double crochet into each two-chain space to make six petals. Join with a slip stitch into the first double crochet and fasten off the yarn.

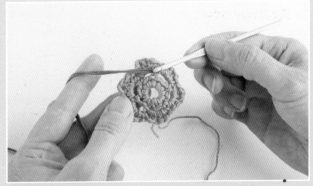

4 Join yarn B to any double crochet in the second round, inserting the hook from the back and around the stem of the stitch.

5 Follow the instructions for the fourth and fifth rounds to complete the flower.

6 The finished flower will have a three-dimensional petal effect.

Folk-art cushion

Bright colours and naïve motifs make this cushion
stand out from the crowd.

This colourful oblong cushion is embellished with stylised appliqué flowers on a half treble background to give it a popular naïve quality.

GETTING STARTED

Individual elements are easy to make but care is needed with assembly for a good result.

Size:
To fit a 45 x 35cm (18 x 14in) cushion pad

How much yarn:
4 x 50g (1¾oz) balls of Debbie Bliss Baby Cashmerino in colour A – jade (shade 044)
Small amounts in each of seven contrast colours:
B – Bright Green (shade 47); C – Llight Green (shade 002); D – Turquoise (shade 46); E – Pink (shade 042); F – Red (shade 034); G – Lilac (shade 033) and H – Cream (shade 101)

Hook:
4.00mm (UK 8) crochet hook

Additional item:
Tapestry needle

Tension:
19 sts and 14 rows measure 10cm (4in) square over htr on 4.00mm (UK 8) hook
IT IS ESSENTIAL TO WORK TO THE STATED TENSION TO ACHIEVE SUCCESS

What you have to do:
Work back and front of cushion in rows of half trebles. Make individual flower motifs with stems and leaves as directed. Sew motifs to cushion front. Crochet back and front of cushion together.

 Instructions

BACK:
With 4.00mm (UK 8) hook and A, make 81ch.
Foundation row: 1htr in 3rd ch from hook, 1htr in each ch to end, turn.
Patt row: 2ch (counts as first htr), miss st at base of ch, 1htr in each htr to end, working last htr in 2nd of 2ch, turn. 80htr.
Rep last row to form patt until work measures 33cm (13in) from beg. Fasten off.

FRONT:
Work as given for Back.

BLUE AND PINK FLOWER:
Flower: With 4.00mm (UK 8) hook and D, make a magic circle as foll: wrap yarn twice clockwise around forefinger to form a ring. Holding end of yarn between thumb and middle finger, insert hook in ring and draw yarn from ball through. Do not pull up centre ring until 1st round has been worked.

The Yarn
Debbie Bliss Baby Cashmerino (approx. 125m/ 136 yards per 50g/1¾oz ball) is a blend of 55% merino wool, 33% microfibre and 12% cashmere. It produces a soft, luxurious fabric, machine-washable at a low temperature. There is a large shade range.

1st round: 3ch, leaving last loop of each on hook, work 2tr in ring, yrh and draw through all 3 loops on hook (first cluster worked), *3ch, leaving last loop of each on hook, work 3tr in ring, yrh and draw through all 4 loops on hook – cluster (cl) formed, rep from * 8 times more, join with a tr in top of first cl, joining on E on last part of st. Cut off D.

2nd round: With E, 3ch, leaving last loop of each on hook, work 2tr in first sp, yrh and draw through all 3 loops on hook, *5ch, 1cl in next sp, rep from * 8 times more, 1ch, join with a dtr in top of first cl, joining on D on last part of st. Cut off E.

3rd round: 1ch (does not count as a st), 6dc in each 5ch loop all round, join with a ss in first dc.

4th round: 1ch, 1dc in each of first 3dc, 3ch, 6dc in each of next 3dc, *1dc in each of next 3dc, 3ch, 1dc in each of foll 3dc, rep from * 8 times more, join with a ss in first ch. Fasten off.

Stem: With 4.00mm (UK 8) hook and B double,

make an 18cm (7in) length of ch. Fasten off.

Leaves: (make 4)
With 4.00mm (UK 8) hook and B, make 12ch.
Working in top loop only, work 1dc in 2nd ch from hook, 1dc in next ch, *1htr in each of next 2ch, 1tr in each of next 3ch, 1htr in each of next 2ch, 1dc in each of last 2ch *, do not turn but work along other side of ch, 1dc in each of first 2ch, rep from * to *, join with a ss in first ch. Fasten off.

STRIPED FLOWER:
Flower: With 4.00mm (UK 8) hook and F, make 8ch.
Foundation row: (RS) 1htr in 3rd ch from hook, 1htr in each ch to end, turn. 7 sts.
Joining on and cutting off colours as required, work in stripes of 1 row each G and F, shaping as foll:
Inc row: 2ch (counts as first htr), 1htr in st at base of ch, 1htr in each htr to end, 2htr in 2nd of 2ch, turn. 9htr.
Rep last row 3 times more. 15htr.
Work straight until 5th stripe in F has been worked. Cut off G.
Next row: (WS) 3ch, 2tr in st at base of

ch, 3tr in each htr to end, working last 3tr in 2nd of 2ch. Fasten off.

Stem: With 4.00mm (UK 8) hook and C, make a 21cm (8¼in) length of chain.
Fasten off.

Leaves: (make 4)

With 4.00mm (UK 8) hook and C, make 9ch.
Working in top loop only, work 1dc in 2nd ch from hook, 1dc in next ch, *1htr in next ch, 1tr in each of next 2ch, 1htr in next ch, 1dc in each of last 2ch *, do not turn but work along other side of ch, 1dc in each of first 2ch, rep from * to *, join with a ss in first ch. Fasten off.

SMALL BLUE FLOWER:

With 4.00mm (UK 8) hook and D, make a magic circle.

1st round: 1ch (counts as first dc), 5dc in ring, join with a ss in first ch.

2nd round: 1ch, 1dc in dc at base of ch, 2dc in each dc all round, join with a ss in first ch. 12 sts.

3rd round: 2ch (counts as first htr), 2htr in next dc, *1htr in next dc, 2htr in next dc, rep from * all round, join with a ss in 2nd of 2ch. 18 sts.

4th round: 2ch, 1htr in next htr, 2htr in next htr, *1htr in each of next 2htr, 2htr in next htr, rep from * all round, join with with a ss in 2nd of 2ch. 24 sts. Fasten off.

THREE-COLOUR FLOWER:

Flower: With 4.00mm (UK 8) hook and B, make a magic circle.

1st round: 3ch (counts as first tr), 1tr in ring, *2ch, 2tr in ring, rep from * 4 times more, 1ch, join with a dc in 3rd of 3ch, joining on G on last part of st. Cut off B.

2nd round: 4ch, *(1tr, 2ch, 1tr) in next sp, 1ch, rep from * 4 times more, 1tr in last sp, join with a htr in 3rd of 4ch.

3rd round: 3ch, (1tr, 2ch, 2tr) in first sp, 1dc in next 1ch sp, *(2tr, 2ch, 2tr) in next 2ch sp, 1dc in next 1ch sp, rep from * all round, join with a ss in 3rd of 3ch, joining on E on last part of st. Cut off G.

4th round: 3ch, *(3tr, 3ch, 3tr) in next 2ch sp, 1tr in next tr, miss next tr, 1dc in next dc, miss next tr, 1tr in next tr, rep from * all round, omitting last tr, join with a ss in 3rd of 3ch. Fasten off.

Stem: With 4.00mm (UK 8) hook and B double, make an 18cm (7in) length of ch. Fasten off.

Leaves: (make 4)

With 4.00mm (UK 8) hook and H, make 14ch.
Working in top loop only, work ss in 2nd ch from hook, 1dc in each of next 2ch, 1tr in each of next 3ch, 1dtr in

each of next 3ch, 1tr in each of next 2ch, 1dc in next ch, ss in last ch, do not turn but work along other side of ch, ss in first ch, 1dc in next ch, 1tr in each of next 2ch, 1dtr in each of next 3ch, 1tr in each of next 3ch, 1dc in each of next 2ch, ss in next ch, join with a ss in first ch. Fasten off.

SMALL FLOWERS:

With 4.00mm (UK 8) hook and B, make a magic circle.

1st round: 1ch (does not count as a st), 12dc in ring, join with a ss in first dc. 12dc.

2nd round: 1ch, (1dc, 5ch, 1dc) in first dc, *1ch, miss next dc, (1dc, 5ch, 1dc) in next dc, rep from * 4 times more, 1ch, join with a ss in first dc.

3rd round: 1ch, (1dc, 1htr, 4tr, 1htr, 1dc) in each 5ch sp all round, join with a ss in first dc. Fasten off.
Make 2 more flowers using E instead of B.

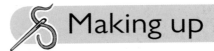

Making up

With 4.00mm (UK 8) hook, WS of Front and Back facing and working into both pieces, join A to top right-hand corner. Working 3dc in each corner, work a row of dc evenly along top, side and lower edges to join pieces; do not fasten off yarn. Insert cushion pad and pin opening closed.

Using tapestry needle and E, work 9 French knots around small blue flower, wrapping yarn twice around needle. Using tapestry needle and F, work a long stitch along centre of each cream (H) leaf, then work a French knot near rounded tip, wrapping yarn twice around needle. Pin flowers, stems (with reverse of ch uppermost) and leaves to front of cushion as shown in photograph, then remove pins from opening and carefully remove cushion pad. Sew flowers and leaves in place, sewing along base of frill on striped flower and about 1cm (⅜in) from outer edge of other flowers; sew along centre of green leaves and along centre and around outer edge of cream leaves. Insert cushion pad and cont to join last side, ss in first dc and fasten off.

Hippy belt

Bring flower power back with this bright tasselled belt to wrap around your jeans.

Hug your hips with this colourful retro-looking belt featuring linked flower motifs and chain ties with bead-trimmed tassels.

GETTING STARTED

⭐ *Belt consists of simple flower motifs and ties.*

Size:

To fit: *small[medium:large]*

Actual length: *approximately 80[90:100]cm (31[35:39]in) (flowers only, minus ties)*

Tie length *approximately 45cm (18in)*

Note: *Figures in square brackets [ ] refer to larger sizes; where there is only one set of figures, it applies to all sizes. It is possible to alter length of belt to fit required size by adding or subtracting flowers*

How much yarn:

1 x 50g (1¾oz) ball of Debbie Bliss Cashmerino DK in each of five colours: A – Teal (shade 19); B – Magenta (shade 37); C – Lime (shade 25); D – Bright Pink (shade 22) and E – Purple (shade 36)

Hook:

4.00mm (UK 8) crochet hook

Additional items:

4 x plastic pony beads and 4 x plastic faceted beads in assorted colours

Tension:

Each flower measures approximately 5cm (2in) in diameter on 4.00mm (UK 8) hook

IT IS ESSENTIAL TO WORK TO THE STATED TENSION TO ACHIEVE SUCCESS

What you have to do:

Work a series of flower motifs in the round, with inner round in one colour and outer round in a second colour. Sew motifs together side by side for belt. At each end of belt make two chain and slip stitch ties. Decorate ends of ties with beads and multi-coloured tassels.

The Yarn
Debbie Bliss Cashmerino DK (approx. 125m/136 yards per 50g/1¾oz ball) contains 55% merino wool, 33% microfibre and 12% cashmere. It is machine washable at a low temperature and there is a wide range of shades.

Instructions

Abbreviations:

ch = chain

cm = centimetre(s)

dc = double crochet

foll = follows

rep = repeat

RS = right side

ss = slip stitch

st(s) = stitch(es)

tr2tog = work 1tr into each of next 2 sts leaving last loop of each on hook, yarn round hook and draw through all 3 loops

BELT:
Flower:

With 4.00mm (UK 8) hook and first colour, make 6ch, join with a ss into first ch to form a ring.

1st round: Work 18dc into ring, join with a ss into first dc. Fasten off.

2nd round: Join second colour to same place as ss, *3ch, tr2tog over next 2 dc, 3ch, ss into next dc, rep from * 5 times more, working last ss into first dc of previous round. Fasten off.

Make 16[17:18] flowers in total in colours as foll:

2[3: 3] with C at centre and D outside

2[2: 3] with A at centre and B outside

2[2: 2] with C at centre and E outside

2[2: 2] with B at centre and D outside

2[2: 2] with C at centre and B outside

2[2: 2] with D at centre and E outside

2[2: 2] with B at centre and A outside

2[2: 2] with E at centre and C outside

Making up

Darn in all ends. Place flower motifs in order required and sew them together through the edges of two adjoining petals.

Ties:

With 4.00mm (UK 8) hook and RS of work facing, join D between tr2tog of one end petal of flower at one end of belt and make 75ch. Fasten off.

Next row: Join in E to last ch worked, I ss into each ch to end, ss into flower petal. Fasten off.

Repeat to make a tie on other end petal of same flower and then on two end petals of flower at other end of belt.

Darn in yarn ends at flower end of ties but leave yarn ends at other end for attaching beads and tassels. Thread a pony bead, then a faceted bead onto each tie and knot yarn ends to secure.

Tassels:

Cut a 14cm (5½in) length of each yarn colour and place together in a bundle. Fold bundle of yarns in half and, using yarn ends beyond beads, tie around with a knot under bundle. Using another length of yarn, tie around bundle to form a tassel and knot to secure. Trim tassel to an even length. Repeat to make a tassel trim on other three ties.

Mini corsages

Pin these corsages to your hat, jacket or jumper or attach them to a bag. They are fun and funky and addictive to make!

Style an outfit quickly and easily with these little corsages in a trio of background and flower shapes held together with a coloured button at their centre. They are such fun that you can make lots of them in pick 'n' mix colours.

The Yarn

Patons 100% Cotton DK (approx. 210m/229 yards per 100g/3½oz ball) is a pure cotton yarn. It has a slight twist and subtle sheen that produces good-looking stitches and fabrics. There are plenty of contemporary colours, which are ideal for mix 'n' match colour work.

GETTING STARTED

 Simple way for a beginner to practise working small motifs.

Size:

Round flower corsage: 7cm (2¾in) in diameter

Square daisy corsage: 7cm (2¾in) square

Hexagonal corsage: 7cm (2¾in) in diameter

How much yarn:

1 x 100g (3½oz) ball of Patons 100% Cotton DK in each of seven colours: A – Cheeky (shade 02719); B – Candy (shade 02734); C – Lilac (shade 02701); D – Grape (shade 02733); E – Rosewood (shade 02720); F – Kiwi (shade 02703) and G – Moss (shade 02731)

Hook:

3.00mm (UK 11) crochet hook

Additional items:

1 button for centre of each corsage

Sewing needle and thread

1 safety-pin for each corsage

Tension:

See 'Size' above

What you have to do:

Work flower separately in rounds using one of five colours. Work background motif separately in rounds using one of two green shades. Place flower on its background and sew button to the centre. Attach safety-pin to corsage back if required.

Instructions

Abbreviations:

bobble = work 5tr into next st leaving last loop of each on hook, yrh and draw through all 6 loops;

ch = chain(s)

cm = centimetre(s)

cluster = work 3tr into next st leaving last loop of each on hook, yrh and draw through all 4 loops

dc = double crochet

htr = half treble

rep = repeat

sp(s) = space(s)

ss = slip stitch

st(s) = stitch(es)

tog = together

tr = treble

tr2tog = work 1tr into each of next 2 sts leaving last loop of each on hook, yrh and draw through all 3 loops

yrh = yarn round hook

ROUND FLOWER CORSAGE:
Flower:

With 3.00mm (UK 11) hook and A, B, C, D or E, make 6ch, join with a ss into first ch to form a ring.

1st round: 1ch, work 15dc into ring, join with a ss into first dc.

2nd round: (3ch, tr2tog, 3ch, ss into next dc) 5 times. Fasten off.

Background:

With 3.00mm (UK 11) hook and F or G, make 6ch, join with a ss into first ch to form a ring.

1st round: 3ch (counts as first tr), work 15tr into ring, join with a ss into 3rd of 3ch.

2nd round: 5ch (counts as first tr and 2ch), 1tr into st at base of ch, (1ch, miss 1tr, into next tr work 1tr, 2ch and 1tr) 7 times, 1ch, join with a ss into 3rd of 5ch.

3rd round: 2ch (counts as first htr), 2tr and 1htr into next 2ch sp, 1dc into next 1ch sp, (1htr, 2tr and 1htr into next 2ch sp, 1dc into next 1ch sp) 7 times, join with a ss into same place as 2ch. Fasten off.

SQUARE DAISY CORSAGE:
Daisy:

With 3.00mm (UK 11) hook and A, B, C, D or E, make 6ch, join with a ss into first ch to form a ring.

1st round: 1ch, (work 1dc into ring, 12ch) 12 times, join with a ss into first dc. Fasten off.

Background:

With 3.00mm (UK 11) hook and F or G, make 4ch, join with a ss into first ch to form a ring.

1st round: 5ch (counts as first tr and 2ch), (3tr into ring, 2ch) 3 times, 2tr into ring, join with a ss into 3rd of 5ch.

2nd round: Ss into next ch sp, 5ch, 3tr into same sp, (1ch, miss next 3tr, into next 2ch sp work 3tr, 2ch and 3tr) 3 times, 1ch, miss next 3tr, 2tr into same sp as 5ch, join with a ss into 3rd of 5ch.

3rd round: Ss into next ch sp, 5ch, 3tr into same sp, (1ch, miss next 3tr, 3tr into next ch sp, 1ch, miss next 3tr, into next 2ch sp work 3tr, 2ch and 3tr)

3 times, 1ch, miss next 3tr, 3tr into next ch sp, 1ch, miss next 3tr, 2tr into same sp as 5ch, join with a ss into 3rd of 5ch. Fasten off.

HEXAGONAL CORSAGE:

Flower:

With 3.00mm (UK 11) hook and A, B, C, D or E, make 6ch, join with a ss into first ch to form a ring.

1st round: 1ch, work 12dc into ring, join with a ss into first dc.

2nd round: 3ch, into st at base of ch work 4tr leaving last loop of each on hook, yrh and draw through all 5 loops on hook, (5ch, miss 1dc, 1 bobble into next dc) 5 times, 5ch, miss 1dc, join with a ss into top of first bobble. Fasten off.

Background:

With 3.00mm (UK 11) hook and F or G, make 5ch, join with a ss into first ch to form a ring.

1st round: 3ch, (1 cluster into ring, 2ch) 6 times, join with a ss into top of first cluster.

2nd round: Ss into first 2ch sp, 3ch, work (1 cluster, 2ch

and 1 cluster) into first 2ch sp, 2ch, *into next 2ch sp work (1cluster, 2ch and 1 cluster, 2ch)rep from * to end, join with a ss into top of first cluster.

3rd round: Ss into first 2ch sp, 1ch (counts as first dc), 2dc into same sp, *(3dc, 2ch and 3dc) into next 2ch sp, 3dc into next ch sp, rep from * 4 times more, (3dc, 2ch and 3dc) into final ch sp, join with a ss into first ch. Fasten off.

Making up

Place flower on top of its background, matching centres, and, using thread to match flower, sew button in place to secure. If required, attach safety-pin to back of corsage.

Floral medallion scarf

A striking accessory, this scarf adds the lightest of touches to an evening outfit.

Worked in a soft mohair yarn, this unusual scarf comprises small floral motifs joined together with a cobweb of chain stitches. The motifs at each end are trimmed with a knotted fringe.

The Yarn

Rowan Kidsilk Haze (approx. 210m/229 yards per 25g/1oz ball) is a blend of 70% super kid mohair and 30% silk. It produces a luxuriously soft, brushed fabric. It is hand-wash only in cool water. There is a fabulous palette of colours.

GETTING STARTED

Very easy motifs but working with mohair yarn and joining requires patience.

Size:
Finished size approximately 15 x 160cm (6 x 63in) (excluding fringe) when laid out flat

How much yarn:
2 x 25g (1oz) balls of Rowan Kidsilk Haze in Splendour (shade 579)

Hook:
3.50mm (UK 9) crochet hook

Tension:
One motif measures 4cm (1½in) in diameter on 3.50mm (UK 9) hook using two strands of yarn

What you have to do:
Make 53 simple floral medallions, working in the round. Using assembly diagram as a guide, join medallions together with lengths of chain. Add a fringe to each end of scarf.

Instructions

Abbreviations:

ch = chain(s)
cm = centimetre(s)
ss = slip stitch
tr = treble

FLORAL MEDALLION: (make 53)

With 3.50mm (UK 9) hook and two strands of yarn, make 6ch, join with a ss into first ch to form a ring.

1st round: (RS) (3ch, 3tr into ring, 3ch, ss into ring) 4 times. Fasten off.

Sew in loose ends neatly.

Making up

Using assembly diagram as a guide, lay out first 8 medallions on a flat surface, making sure RS is uppermost on each medallion. With 3.50mm (UK 9) hook and two strands of yarn, join medallions with lengths of ch, following direction of arrows on diagram:

Join yarn with a ss into centre tr of lower petal on medallion 1, make 22ch, join with a ss into centre tr of top petal on medallion 2; make 10ch, join with a ss into centre tr of lower petal on medallion 3; make 10ch, join with a ss into centre tr of upper petal on medallion

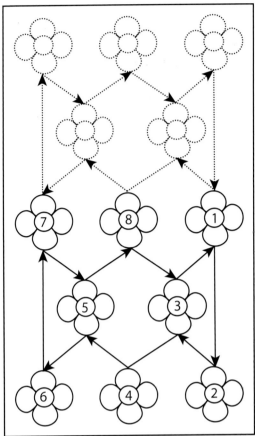

4; make 10ch, join with a ss into centre tr of lower petal on medallion 5; make 10ch, join with a ss into centre tr of upper petal on medallion 6; make 22ch, join with a ss into centre tr of lower petal on medallion 7; make 10ch, join with a ss into centre tr of upper petal on medallion 5; make 10ch, join with a ss into centre tr of lower petal on medallion 8; make 10ch, join with a ss into centre tr of upper petal on medallion 3; make 10ch, join with a ss into same place as first ss on medallion 1. Fasten off. Using assembly diagram as a guide, continue to add 5 medallions at a time until all 53 medallions have been attached.

Note: To make a longer scarf, simply add medallions in multiples of 5. Each set of 5 medallions adds approximately 15cm (6in) to length of scarf.

Fringe:
Cut 36 x 30cm (12in) lengths of yarn. Taking 6 lengths together for each tassel, fold in half and knot through centre tr of lower petal of one medallion at end of scarf. Knot a tassel in each of three medallions at each end of scarf.

Trio of bracelets

A perfect project for the crochet beginner, these summer bracelets would make a great homemade gift.

Designed to be worn separately or all three together, these stylish bracelets are worked in 4-ply cotton in coordinating colours, using simple stitches and decorated with pretty buttons.

The Yarn

Rowan Siena 4-ply (approx. 140m/153 yards per 50g/1¾oz ball) is a smooth 100% cotton yarn in a 4-ply weight. When worked with a smaller hook than recommended, it produces a firm fabric. There is a large colour range.

GETTING STARTED

 These bracelets make good projects for beginners.

Size:

To fit an average-sized woman's wrist

Actual circumference: Flower band 19.5–22.5cm (7¾–9in) (adjustable); Button bracelet 20.5cm (8in) and Bangle 20.5cm (8in)

How much yarn:

1 x 50g (1¾oz) ball of Rowan Siena in each of three colours: A – Pacific (shade 660); B – Rosette (shade 664) and C – Grasshopper (shade 663)

Hook:

2.25mm (UK 13) crochet hook

Additional items:

2 x 12mm (½in) ribbon end crimps

2 x 5mm (¼in) jump rings

1 x small bolt ring

3cm (1¼in) of chain

Wire bangle, 6.5cm (2½in) diameter

1 x 11mm (½in) mother-of-pearl round button

11 x 11mm (½in) mother-of-pearl flower-shaped buttons

Flat-nosed pliers

What you have to do:

For Flower band, crochet flower and band separately and sew together. Finish ends with metal crimps and a chain-and-ring fastening that can be adjusted. For Button bracelet, work a row of shells on either side of foundation chain to create a scallop-edged band and finish with a button-and-loop fastening. Sew on flower-shaped buttons to each shell. For Bangle, use an inexpensive, thin metal bangle as a base and cover it with rounds of double crochet. Sew on a button to neaten place where rounds are joined.

Instructions

Abbreviations:
ch = chain(s)
cm = centimetre(s)
dc = double crochet
dtr4tog = work 4dtr into same dc leaving last loop of each on hook, yrh and draw through all 5 loops
rep = repeat
RS = right side
ss = slip stitch
st(s) = stitch(es)
tog = together
tr = treble
yrh = yarn round hook

FLOWER BAND:
Flower:
With 2.25mm (UK 13) hook and A, make 6ch, join with a ss into first ch to form a ring.
1st round: 1ch (counts as first dc), work 14dc into ring, join with a ss into first ch. Fasten off A.
2nd round: Join B to same place as ss, 1ch, 1dc into next dc, *3ch, dtr4tog into next dc, 3ch, 1dc into each of next 2dc, rep from * 3 times more, 3ch, dtr4tog into next dc, 3ch, join with a ss into first ch. Fasten off B, leaving a tail of yarn for attaching to band.

Band:
With 2.25mm (UK 13) hook and B, make 40ch to measure 18cm (7in).
1st row: 1dc into 2nd ch from hook, 1dc into each ch to end, turn.
2nd row: 1ch (counts as 1dc), 1dc into each dc to end, turn.
3rd row: As 2nd row. Fasten off.

BUTTON BRACELET:
With 2.25mm (UK 13) hook and C, make 45ch to measure 21cm (8¼in).
1st round: 1dc into 5th ch from hook to make button loop, (miss 1ch, 5tr into next ch, miss 1ch, 1dc into next ch) 9 times, 1dc into each of last 4ch, do not turn. Working into opposite side of foundation ch, work 1dc into each of first 5ch, (miss 1ch, 5tr into next ch, miss 1ch, 1dc into

next ch) 9 times, work 1ss and 6dc into button loop, join with a ss into first ch of round. Fasten off.

BANGLE:

(Worked throughout with back facing)

Foundation round: Attach A to bangle, with 2.25mm (UK 13) hook, work 1ch (counts as first dc), 79dc over bangle, join with a ss into first ch.

1st round: 1ch, 1dc into each dc to end, inserting hook into back loop only, join with a ss into first ch.

2nd round: As 1st round, inserting hook into front loop only of sts of foundation round.

3rd round: 1ch, insert hook through back loop of first st of 2nd round then through back loop of first st of 1st round, yrh and draw loop through, yrh and draw through 2 loops on hook – joining dc worked, (work joining dc into back loop of next dc of 2nd round and next dc of 1st round) to end, join with a ss into first ch. Fasten off.

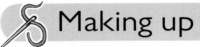 Making up

BUTTON BRACELET:

Using sewing needle and thread to match button, sew one flower-shaped button to centre of each double shell and one button to end of bracelet opposite button loop.

FLOWER BAND:

Sew flower to centre of band, using tail of yarn, then sew round button to centre of flower. Attach one ribbon end crimp to each end of band and attach bolt ring to one crimp, using one jump ring, and chain to other crimp, using remaining jump ring.

BANGLE:

With RS facing, sew on a flower-shaped button to cover joining of rounds.

Flower corsage tote bag

Choose a bright lining fabric and coordinating yarn for this big bold bag.

This stylish bag is worked in a textured pattern with a contrast-coloured deep border at the top featuring a floral corsage. The interior is lined in a printed fabric and the bag has matching fabric handles.

GETTING STARTED

Main crochet fabric takes practice and neat sewing skills are required for a professional finish.

Size:
Finished bag measures 33cm (13in) wide x 40cm (15¾in) deep, excluding handles

How much yarn:
2 x 100g (3½oz) balls of Sirdar Supersoft Aran in colour A – Blue (shade 827)
1 ball in colour B – Cream (shade 831)

Hook:
5.00mm (UK 6) crochet hook

Additional items:
90 x 50cm (36 x 20in) piece of printed cotton fabric for lining
1 x 2cm (¾in) domed shank button
Sewing needle and matching thread

Tension:
13 sts and 12 rows measure 10cm (4in) square over patt on 5.00mm (UK 6) hook
IT IS ESSENTIAL TO WORK TO THE STATED TENSION TO ACHIEVE SUCCESS

What you have to do:
Work main part of bag in one colour in textured pattern with relief double trebles. Work border at top of bag in second colour in rib pattern. Make circular flower motif for corsage and trim with fabric-covered button. Sew fabric lining and handles for bag.

The Yarn
Sirdar Supersoft Aran (approx. 236m/257 yards per 100g/3½oz ball) contains 100% acrylic. It makes a soft, yet strong fabric. It can be machine washed and there is a wide range of colours.

Instructions

Abbreviations:

beg = beginning

ch = chain

cm = centimetre(s)

cont = continue

dc = double crochet

dtr = double treble

foll = follow(s)(ing)

htr = half treble

patt = pattern

rep = repeat

RS = right side

rdtrf = relief dtr front: inserting hook from right to left and from front to back, work 1dtr around stem of st indicated

ss = slip stitch

st(s) = stitch(es)

tr = treble

WS = wrong side

BAG:

With 5.00mm (UK 6) hook and A, make 86ch loosely, join with a ss into first ch to form a loop, taking care not to twist ch.

1st round: 3ch (counts as first tr), miss st at base of ch, 1tr into each ch to end, join with a ss into 3rd of 3ch. 86 sts.

2nd round: 1ch (counts as first dc), miss st at base of ch, 1dc into each st to end, join with a ss into first ch.

3rd round: 3ch, miss st at base of ch, (1rdtrf around stem of next tr 2 rounds below, miss one st, 1tr into foll st) 42 times, 1rdtrf around stem of next tr 2 rounds below, join with a ss into 3rd of 3ch.

4th round: As 2nd.

5th round: Ss into next st, 3ch, miss st at base of ch, (1rdtrf around stem of next tr 2 rounds below, miss one st, 1tr into foll st) 42 times, 1rdtrf around stem of next tr 2 rounds below, join with a ss into 3rd

of 3ch. Rep 4th and 5th rounds to form patt until work measures 32cm (00in) from beg, ending with a 5th round and joining in B on last part of last st. Cut off A.

Border:

Cont with B as foll: Work 4th and 5th rounds once, then work 4th round again.

Next round: 3ch, miss st at base of ch, (1rdtrf around stem of next rdtrf 2 rounds below, miss next st, 1tr in foll st) 42 times, 1rdtrf around stem of next rdtrf 2 rounds below, join with a ss into 3rd of 3ch.

Next round: As 4th round.

Rep last 2 rounds 3 more times. Fasten off.

FLOWER CORSAGE:

With 5.00mm (UK 6) hook and A, make 9ch, join with a ss into first ch to form a ring.

1st round: 1ch (counts as first dc), work 15dc into ring, join with a ss into first ch.

2nd round: 7ch (counts as first tr and 4ch, miss next dc, (1tr into foll dc, 4ch, miss next dc) 7 times, join with a ss into 3rd of 7ch.

3rd round: Into each 4ch loop all round, work (1htr, 1tr, 1dtr, 1ch, 1dtr, 1tr, 1htr, 1ss). Fasten off.

Cut a circle of fabric to twice diameter of button. Sew a round of small running sts around outer edge, then draw up thread. Slip button inside gathered fabric and pull up thread tightly. Fasten off securely, then sew button to centre of flower.

Making up

Join seam at lower edge of bag.

From printed lining fabric, cut out one 68 x 45cm (27 x 17¾in) rectangle for lining bag and two 10 x 42cm (4 x 17in) strips for handles. Fold two handle strips in half lengthways, with RS facing, and machine-stitch 1cm (⅜in) from long edges. Turn RS out and press so that seam lies along one edge. Fold bag lining in half widthways with RS facing. Pin, then machine-stitch along side and lower edge, taking 1cm (⅜in) seam allowances. Press seam allowances inwards, then press back a 5cm (2in) turning around top opening edge.

Pin handles to WS of top opening edge, so that ends lie 8cm (3⅛in) in from corners and overlap fold by 1cm (⅜in). Machine-stitch two rounds around top opening edge, 3mm (⅛in) and 6mm (¼in) from fold. Slide lining inside bag and neatly slip stitch in place around top of bag, then with lining uppermost, work a round of machine-stitching 1.5cm (⅝in) down from top edge to hold lining in position.

Sew on corsage as shown in photograph.

Flower scarf

Make a stylish floral statement with this bold colourful scarf.

Formed from a series of individual flower motifs that have been joined together, this colourful scarf is defined with a chain and mesh edging.

The Yarn

Debbie Bliss Fez (approx. 100m/109 yards per 50g/1¾oz ball) contains 85% merino wool and 15% camel. It is an aran-weight yarn, extremely soft and luxurious but washable with care at a low temperature. There is a good range of colours.

GETTING STARTED

★ ★ *Motifs are easy to work but careful construction is essential.*

Size:
Finished scarf measures approximately 20cm (8in) wide x 132cm (52in) long, excluding tassels

How much yarn:
3 x 50g (1¾oz) balls of Debbie Bliss Fez in colour A – Green (shade 06)
1 ball in each of three colours: B – Fucshia (shade 12); C – Rose (shade 13) and D – Pale Blue (shade 14)

Hook:
5.00mm (UK 6) crochet hook

Tension:
Each flower motif is 12cm (4¾in) in diameter on 5.00mm (UK 6) hook
IT IS ESSENTIAL TO WORK TO THE STATED TENSION TO ACHIEVE SUCCESS

What you have to do:
Make individual flower motifs, varying colours of flower centres. Sew tips of petals together to form scarf. Work chain edging around outer edge and rows of mesh edging at each short end. Knot tassels through loops in edging.

Instructions

Abbreviations:

ch = chain
dc = double crochet
dtr = double treble
foll = follows
htr = half treble
rep = repeat
RS = right side
sp = space
ss = slip stitch
tr = treble
WS = wrong side

SCARF:
Fower motif:

With 5.00mm (UK 6) hook and B, make 6ch.

1st round: Into 6th ch from hook, work (1tr, 2ch) 7 times, join with a ss into 3rd of 5ch. Fasten off B.

2nd round: Join C to any 2ch sp, 1ch (counts as first dc) *(5ch, ss into 4th ch from hook – picot made) twice, 1ch, 1dc into next 2ch sp, rep from * to end, omitting 1dc at end of last rep, join with a ss into first ch. Fasten off C.

3rd round: Working behind sts of last round, join A to 2 strands at back of any dc in previous round, *6ch, ss into 2 strands at back of next dc of previous round, rep from * to end, working last ss into 2 strands at back of first dc.

4th round: With A, work * (1dc, 1htr, 4tr, 1dtr, 4tr, 1htr

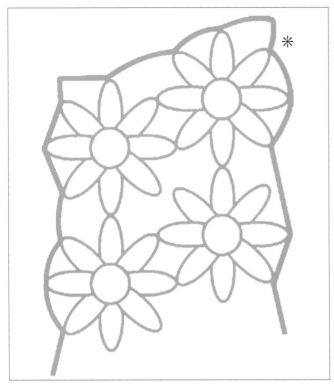

and 1dc) all into next 6ch loop, 1dc into next ss, rep from * to end. Fasten off.

Work 19 more motifs, varying colours of 1st and 2nd rounds and always working 3rd and 4th rounds with A.

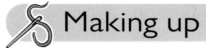

Making up

Using diagram as a guide, sew motifs together in pairs through points on petals.

Edging:

With 5.00mm (UK 6) hook and RS of work facing, join A to dtr at centre of lower right petal of right-hand motif at one short end of Scarf (marked with * on diagram) and work all round as foll: **10ch for corner, (ss into dtr at centre of next petal of same motif, 6ch) twice, ss into dtr at centre of first petal on next motif, 10ch for corner, ss into dtr at centre of next petal, *6ch, ss into dtr at centre of next free edge petal*, rep from * to * along long edge of Scarf until ss has been worked into 3rd free petal on last motif (marked with * on diagram), rep from ** once. Fasten off and turn work. Now work mesh edging along one short end as foll:

1st row: With WS facing, join A to 5th ch of 10ch loop at right corner of short end, 6ch, 1dc into 10ch loop, (6ch, 1dc into 6ch loop) twice, 6ch, 1dc into 10ch loop, 3ch, 1tr into 5th of 10ch, turn.

2nd row: 1ch, 1dc into tr, (6ch, 1dc into next 6ch loop) 3 times, 6ch, 1dc into 4th of 6ch, turn.

3rd row: (6ch, 1dc into 6ch loop) 4 times, 3ch, 1tr into dc, turn.

4th row: As 2nd row. Fasten off.

Work mesh edging along other short end to match.

Tassels: (make 18)

For each tassel, cut 5 x 40cm (16in) lengths of A. Fold strands in half and hook folded end through dc at corner of one short edge. Pass cut ends of yarn through loop and pull to tighten. Knot one tassel into each dc and into centre of each ch loop. Trim ends.

Flower-edged jacket

Mini sunflowers edge this soft, mesh-patterned jacket.

Edge-to-edge in a simple openwork pattern and beautiful soft yarn, this sweet jacket is trimmed with two-colour flower motifs sewn onto the neckline and front edge.

The Yarn

Artesano Alpaca 4-ply and Artesano Alpaca DK (approx. 100m/109 yards per 50g/1¾oz ball) both contain 100% superfine alpaca. They produce a luxurious soft hand-washable fabric. There is an attractive colour palette featuring bright colours as well as natural shades.

GETTING STARTED

★★ *Pattern is easy to work with practice but take care when sewing motifs on.*

Size:
To fit bust: 81[86:91:97]cm (32[34:36:38]in)
Actual size: 88[96:104:112]cm (34½[37¾:41:44]in)
Length: 55[56:57:57]cm (21½[22:22½:22½]in)
Sleeve seam: 27[27:29.5:29.5]cm (10[10½:15½: 15½]in)
Note: Figures in square brackets [ ] refer to larger sizes; where only one set of figures is given, it applies to all sizes

How much yarn:
10[10:11:12] x 50g (1¾oz) balls of Artesano Alpaca DK in colour A – Cream (shade SFN10)
1 x 50g (1¾oz) ball Artesano Alpaca 4-ply in each of colour B – Ecuador (shade 8774) and colour C – Brazil (shade 5340)

Hooks:
3.50mm (UK 9) crochet hook
4.00mm (UK 8) crochet hook

Tension:
15 sts and 8 rows measure 10cm (4in) square over patt on 4.00mm (UK 8) hook
IT IS ESSENTIAL TO WORK TO THE STATED TENSION TO ACHIEVE SUCCESS

What you have to do:
Work main fabric in openwork pattern featuring alternate rows of treble groups and V stitches. Shape armholes, neckline and sleeves as directed. Work double crochet edging around all outer edges. Make flower and leaf motifs in contrasting colours and use to trim neckline and front edges.

 ## Instructions

BACK:

With 3.50mm (UK 9) hook and A, make 65[71:77:83]ch.
Foundation row: (RS) 1dc in 2nd ch from hook, 1dc in each ch to end, turn. 64[70:76:82]dc.
Next row: 1ch (does not count as a st), 1dc in each dc to end, turn. Rep last row twice more.
Change to 4.00mm (UK 8) hook. Cont in patt as foll:
1st row: (RS) 3ch (counts as first tr), 1tr in st at base of ch, (miss next 2dc, 3tr in next dc) to last 3dc, miss next

2dc, 2tr in last dc, turn. 20[22:24:26] 3tr grs.
2nd row: 3ch, (1tr, 1ch, 1tr – called V-st) in sp before each 3tr gr, V-st in sp after last 3tr gr, 1tr in 3rd of 3ch, turn. 21[23:25:27] V-sts.
3rd row: 3ch, 1tr in sp before first V-st, 3tr in sp before each V-st, 1tr in sp between last V-st and turning ch, 1tr in 3rd of 3ch, turn.
The last 2 rows form patt. Cont in patt until work measures 37cm (14½in) from beg, ending with a WS row.

Abbreviations:

beg = beginning
ch = chain
cm = centimetre(s)
cont = continue
dc = double crochet
dc2tog = (insert hook in next st, yrh and draw loop through) twice, yrh and draw through all 3 loops
gr(s) = group(s)
htr = half treble
inc = increase(d)
LE = left edge
patt = pattern
RE = right edge
rem = remaining
rep = repeat
RS = right side
sp = space
ss = slip stitch
st(s) = stitch(es)
tr = treble
WS = wrong side
yrh = yarn round hook

Shape armholes:

1st row: Ss in each of first 4 sts, 3ch, 1tr in sp before next V-st, 3tr in sp before each V-st, ending 2tr in sp between last 2 V-sts, turn. 18[20:22:24] 3tr grs.

2nd row: 3ch, V-st between 1st and 2nd 3tr grs, patt to end, ending V-st between last two 3tr grs, 1tr in sp after last 3tr grp, turn.

3rd row: As 3rd patt row. 16[18:20:22] 3tr grs. Work straight in patt until armholes measure 18[19:20:20]cm (7[7½:8:8]in) from beg, ending with a RS row. Fasten off.

LEFT FRONT:

With 3.50mm (UK 9) hook and A, make 35[38:41:44]ch. Work Foundation row as given for Back (34[37:40:43]dc) and 3 rows in dc. Change to 4.00mm (UK 8) hook. Cont in patt as given for Back (10[11:12:13] 3tr grs) until Front matches Back to armholes, ending with a WS row.

Shape armhole:

Next row: (RS) Ss in each of first 4 sts, 3ch, 1tr in sp before next V-st, patt to end, turn. 9[10:11:12] 3tr grs.

1st RE dec row: Patt to end, ending V-st between last two 3tr grs,

1tr in sp after last 3tr gr, turn.

2nd RE dec row: As 3rd patt row. 8[9:10:11] 3tr grs. Work straight in patt until armhole measures 5 rows less that Back to shoulder, ending with a WS row.

Shape neck:

Next row: Patt until 5[6:7:8] 3tr grs have been worked, 2tr in sp before next V-st, turn.

1st LE dec row: 3ch, V-st between 1st and 2nd 3tr grs, patt to end, turn.

2nd LE dec row: As 3rd patt row. 4[5:6:7] 3tr grs.

Rep last 2 rows 0[0:1:1] time. 4[5:5:6] 3tr grs. Patt 2[2:0:0] rows. Fasten off.

RIGHT FRONT:

Work as given for Left front to armhole.

Shape armhole:

Next row: (RS) Patt, ending 2tr in sp between last 2 V-sts, turn. 9[10:11:12] 3tr grs. Work 1st and 2nd LE dec rows as given for Left front. 8[9:10:11] 3tr grs. Work straight in patt until armhole measures 5 rows less than Back to shoulder, ending with a WS row. Fasten off yarn and turn.

Shape neck:

Next row: (RS) With RS facing rejoin A to sp between 3rd and 4th V-sts, 3ch, 1tr in same place, patt to end, turn.

5[6:7:8] 3tr grs.
Work 1st and 2nd RE dec rows as given for Left front. 4[5:6:7] 3tr grs.
Rep last 2 rows 0[0:1:1] time. 4[5:5:6] 3tr grs. Patt 2[2:0:0] rows. Fasten off.

SLEEVES: (make 2)

With 3.50mm (UK 9 hook) and A, make 44[47:50:50]ch. Work foundation row as given for Back (43[46:49:49]dc) and 3 rows in dc. Change to 4.00mm (UK 8) hook. Work 6 rows in patt as given for Back. 13[14:15:15] 3tr grs.

1st inc row: 3ch, 2tr in st at base of ch, patt to end, ending 3tr in 3rd of 3ch, turn. 1 st inc at each end.

2nd inc row: 3ch, 1tr in st at base of ch, patt to end, ending 2tr in 3rd of 3ch, turn.

3rd inc row: 3ch, 3tr in sp before each V-st, 3tr in sp after last V-st, 1tr in 3rd of 3ch, turn. 1 st inc at each end.

4th inc row: 4ch, 1tr in sp before first 3tr gr, V-st in sp before each 3tr gr, 1tr in sp after last 3tr gr, 1ch, 1tr in 3rd of 3ch, turn.

5th inc row: 3ch, 1tr in st at base of ch, 3tr in sp before each V-st, 3tr in sp after last V-st, 2tr in 3rd of 4ch, turn. 1st inc at each end. 15[16:17:17] 3tr grs.

6th inc row: As 2nd patt row.
Rep last 6 rows once. 17[18:19:19] 3tr grs.
Patt 2[2:4:4] rows, ending with a WS row.

Shape top:

Work 1st – 3rd rows of Back armhole shaping

(13[14:15:15] 3tr grs), then work 2nd, 1st and 2nd rows again. 8[9:10:10] V sts. Fasten off.

FLOWER AND LEAF MOTIFS:

Flower: (make 10)
With 3.50mm (UK 9) hook and B, make 4ch, join with a ss in first ch to form a ring.

1st round: 1ch (does not count as a st), work 13dc in ring, join with a ss in first dc. Fasten off.

2nd round: Join C to any dc of 1st round, (1dc in dc, 5ch, 1dc in 2nd ch from hook, 1htr in each of next 2ch, 1dc in next ch, 1dc in first dc worked) 13 times to make 13 petals. Fasten off.

Leaves: (make 12)
With 3.50mm (UK 9) hook and B, make 8ch.

1st round: 1dc in 2nd ch from hook, 1dc in each of next 5ch, 3dc in last ch, working back along foundation ch, work 1dc in rem loop of each of next 6ch.

2nd round: 3ch, miss next ch, *1dc in next dc, 1htr in next dc, 1tr in each of next 3dc, 1htr in next dc, 1dc in next dc *, 1dc in next dc, rep from * to * once more, join with a ss in first ch. Fasten off.

Making up

Join shoulder seams. Sew in sleeves, then join side and sleeve seams.

Front and neck edging:

With 3.50mm (UK 9) hook and RS facing, join A to lower corner of right front, 1ch (does not count as a st), work in dc evenly up right front edge (working 1dc in every dc row-end, 2dc in every straight tr row-end with additional sts if necessary around front neck shaping and 3dc in corners), round neck and down left front, turn. Work 3 more rows in dc, working 3dc in centre st at each corner and working dc2tog at inner neck corners if necessary to keep work flat. Fasten off.

Using photograph as a guide, arrange flowers and leaves around front neck edges and down fronts, overlapping edges. Pin, then sew in place.

Floral napkin rings

Decorate your alfresco lunch table with these flower-themed napkin rings.

Show off plain napkins with this set of three-dimensional flower-themed rings worked in easy stitches and fresh spring colours.

The Yarn
DMC Petra No. 3 (approx. 280m/305 yards per 100g/3½oz ball) is a mercerized thread in 100% cotton. It is ideal for crochet projects and produces a good-looking fabric with a slight lustre. There is a large range of colours, some of which are variegated, to choose from.

GETTING STARTED

Flower motifs are a good way to practise crochet as they are small and rings consist of simple double crochet.

Size:
Napkin ring (before joining) measures approximately 17.5cm (7in) wide x 4cm (1½in) deep

How much yarn:
1 x 100g (3½oz) ball of DMC Petra No.3 in each of five colours: A – Lime Green (shade 5907); B – Pale Yellow (shade 5745); C – Dark Yellow (shade 5742); D – Mid Orange (shade 5722) and E – Dark Orange (shade 5608)

Hook:
2.50mm (UK 12) crochet hook

Tension:
25 sts and 25 rows measure 10cm (4in) square over dc on 2.50mm (UK 12) hook
IT IS ESSENTIAL TO WORK TO THE STATED TENSION TO ACHIEVE SUCCESS

What you have to do:
Work three-dimensional flower motifs, either flat or in rounds and a variety of colours, as described. Make band of double crochet for napkin ring. Sew flower motif to napkin ring.

 # Instructions

ROSE RING:
Note: Leave a long tail of yarn at start to use for rolling and sewing rose together.
With 2.50mm (UK 12) hook and A, make 62ch.
Flower:
1st row: 1tr in 5th ch from hook (counts as 1tr, 2ch), *1ch, miss 2ch, (1tr, 2ch, 1tr) in next ch, rep from * to end, turn.
2nd row: 3ch (counts as 1tr), (1tr, 2ch, 2tr) all in first 2ch sp, *(2ch, 2tr) twice in next 2ch sp, rep from * to end, working last rep in 5ch sp at beg of 1st row.
3rd row: With B, ss in each of first 2tr, 2ch (counts as

1htr), (1tr, 1dtr, 3ch, 1dtr, 1tr, 1htr) in first 2ch sp, 1dc in next 2ch sp, *(1htr, 1tr, 1dtr, 3ch, 1dtr, 1tr, 1htr) all in next 2ch sp, 1dc in next 2ch sp)* 5 times. Change to C and rep from * to * 7 times. Change to D, (1htr, 1tr, 2dtr, 3ch, 2dtr, 1tr, 1htr) all in next 2ch sp, 1dc in next 2ch sp) 6 times, (1htr, 1tr, 2dtr, 3ch, 2dtr, 1tr, 1htr) all in last 2ch sp. Fasten off.
Thread long starting tail on a large-eyed yarn needle. Beg at opposite end, tightly roll the rose, then sew securely through starting ch on all layers.
Napkin ring:
With 2.50mm (UK 12) hook and B, make 45ch.

Abbreviations:

beg = beginning
ch = chain
cm = centimetre(s)
dc = double crochet
dc2tog = (insert hook in next st and draw a loop through) twice, yrh and draw through all 3 loops
dec = decrease
dtr = double treble
foll = follows
htr = half treble
rep = repeat
sp = space
ss = slip stitch
st(s) = stitch(es)
tr = treble
yrh = yarn round hook

1st row: 1dc in 2nd ch from hook, 1dc in each ch to end, turn.

2nd row: 1ch (does not count as a st), 1dc in each st to end, turn.

Rep last row 8 times more. Fasten off.

DAISY RING:
Lower petals:

With 2.50mm (UK 12) hook and B, make 8ch, join with a ss in first ch to form a ring.

1st round: 1ch, work 12dc in ring, join with a ss in first dc.**

2nd round: 1ch, 1dc in same place as join, (11ch, 1dc in next dc, 1ch, 1dc in next dc) 5 times, 11ch, 1dc in next dc, 1ch, join with a ss in first dc.

3rd round: (18tr in 11ch loop, ss in 1ch sp) 6 times. Fasten off.

Upper petals:

With 2.50mm (UK 12) hook and C, work as Lower petals to **.

2nd round: 1ch, 1dc in same place as join, (8ch, 1dc in next dc, 1ch, 1dc in next dc) 5 times, 8ch, 1dc in next dc, 1ch, join with a ss in first dc.

3rd round: (12tr in 8ch loop, ss in 1ch sp) 6 times. Fasten off.

Centre:

With 2.50mm (UK 12) hook and E, make 2ch.

1st round: 6dc in 2nd ch from hook, join with a ss in first dc.

2nd round: 1ch, 2dc in each dc to end, join with a ss in first dc.

3rd round: 1ch, 1dc into each dc to end, join with a ss in first dc.

Rep last round 4 times more.

Dec round: 1ch, (dc2tog) 6 times, join with a ss in first dc2tog. Fasten off.

Napkin ring:

With 2.50mm (UK 12) hook and A, work as for Rose napkin ring.

DAFFODIL RING:
Centre:

With 2.50mm (UK 12) hook and B, make 4ch, join with a ss in first ch to form a ring. Work with outside facing as foll:

1st round: 3ch (counts as 1tr), work 11tr in ring, join with a ss in 3rd of 3ch.

2nd round: Working in back loop only of each st, 3ch, miss st at base of ch, 1tr in each tr, join with a ss in 3rd of 3ch.

3rd round: 1ch (counts as 1dc), 1dc in st at base of ch, 2dc in each dc to end, join with a ss in first ch. Fasten off.

Petals:

4th round: With 3rd round at back, join C with a ss to any unworked front loop on 1st round, 1ch, (1ch, miss 1 loop, 1dc in next loop) 5 times, 1ch, miss last loop, join with a ss in first ch.

5th round: (Ss in next 1ch loop, 2ch, 1tr, 1dtr, 1trtr, 1dtr, 1tr, 2ch, 1dc in same loop) 6 times.

6th round: 1ch, *1dc in each of next 2ch, 1dc in each of next 2 sts, (1dc, 4ch, 1dc) in next st, 1dc in each of next 2 sts, 1dc in each of next 2ch, rep from * 5 times, join with a ss in first ch. Fasten off.

Napkin ring:
With 2.50mm (UK 12) hook and E, work as for Rose napkin ring.

CHRYSANTHEMUM RING:
Lower petals:
With 2.50mm (UK 12) hook and E, make 8ch, join with a ss in first ch to form a ring.

1st round: 3ch (counts as 1tr), work 23tr in ring, join with a ss in 3rd of 3ch.**

2nd round: 8ch, work back along ch as foll: 1dc in 2nd ch from hook, 1tr in each of next 4ch, miss next tr on 1st round, 1tr in next tr, (5ch, work back along ch as foll: 1dc in 2nd ch from hook, 1tr in each of next 3ch, 1tr into top of last tr on previous rep, miss next tr on 1st round, 1tr in next tr) 11 times omitting last tr, join with a ss in 2nd of 8ch. Fasten off.

Middle petals:
With 2.50mm (UK 12) hook and D, work as for Lower petals to **.

2nd round: 6ch, work back along ch as foll: 1dc in 2nd ch from hook, 1tr in each of next 4ch, miss next tr on 1st round, 1dc in next tr, (5ch, work back along ch as foll: 1dc in 2nd ch from hook, 1tr in each of next 3ch, 1tr in top of last dc on previous rep, miss next tr on 1st round, 1dc in next tr) 11 times omitting last dc, join with a ss in base of 6ch. Fasten off.

Upper petals:
With 2.50mm (UK 12) hook and B, make 8ch, join with a ss in first ch to form a ring.

1st round: 1ch (counts as 1dc), work 23dc in ring, join with a ss in first ch.

2nd round: 6ch, work back along ch as foll: 1dc in 2nd ch from hook, 1tr in each of next 4ch, miss next dc on 1st round, 1dc in next dc, (5ch, work back along ch as foll: 1dc in 2nd ch from hook, 1tr in each of next 3ch, 1tr in top of last dc on previous rep, miss next dc on 1st round, 1dc in next dc) 11 times omitting last dc, join with a ss in base of 6ch. Fasten off.

Centre:
With 2.50mm (UK 12) hook and A, make 2ch.

1st round: 6dc in 2nd ch from hook, join with a ss in first dc.

2nd round: 5ch (counts as 1dc, 4ch), (1dc in next dc, 4ch) 5 times, join with a ss in 1st of 5ch. Fasten off.

Napkin ring:
With 2.50mm (UK 12) hook and C, work as for Rose napkin ring.

Making up

ROSE RING:
Join row ends of napkin ring to form a band. Sew rose securely to napkin ring on top of join.

DAISY RING:
Join row ends of napkin ring to form a band. Place upper petals over lower petals and sew securely to napkin ring on top of join. Sew centre in place in middle of flower.

DAFFODIL RING:
Join row ends of napkin ring to form a band. Sew flower securely to napkin ring on top of join. Using A and D, work a cluster of French knots in centre of flower.

CHRYSANTHEMUM RING:
Join row ends of napkin ring to form a band. Place three layers of petals together and sew securely to napkin ring on top of join. Sew centre in place in middle of flower.

Felted bag with flower motifs

Soft stripes and pretty added-on flower motifs make this a truly distinctive bag.

Worked in double crochet and soft Shetland yarn, this bucket-shaped bag with long handles is felted for its distinctive fuzzy appearance. The button-trimmed flower motifs with embroidered stems are added afterwards.

The Yarn

Jamieson & Smith 2-ply jumper weight yarn (approx. 114m/ 125 yards per 25g/1oz ball) contains 100% Shetland wool and is traditionally used to knit Fair Isle garments. Used double, it is ideal for felting.

GETTING STARTED

Bag is straightforward to make but felting takes time and patience as results are unpredictable.

Size:

Before felting: Bag is 33cm (13in) high x 42cm (16½in) across widest point x 25cm (10in) across base

After felting and blocking: Bag measures approximately 25cm (10in) high x 40cm (16in) across widest point x 23cm (9in) across base

How much yarn:

6 x 25g (1oz) balls of Jamieson & Smith 2-ply jumper-weight in colour A – Pink (shade 1283)

4 balls in each of colour B – Grey (shade 203) and colour C – Ivory (shade 1A)

1 ball in each of colour D – Raspberry (shade FC22) and colour E – Green (shade 026)

Hook:

4.50mm (UK 7) crochet hook

Additional items:

6 x 19mm (¾in) flat shell buttons

Tension:

16 sts and 15 rows measure 10cm (4in) square over dc using two strands of yarn on 4.50mm (UK 7) hook before felting

What you have to do:

Work bag in double crochet throughout, working in rounds for base and handles and rows for main part. Work main part in stripes, carrying colours not in use up side of work. Make up bag, then felt in washing machine. Make flower motifs and sew on, then embroider stems as instructed.

 Instructions

BAG BASE:

With 4.50mm (UK 7) hook and two strands of A, make 5ch, join with a ss in first ch to form a ring.

Note: Work each st in **back** loop only of previous sts; start each round with 2ch (instead of 1ch – this is important for felting) as indicated to count as first dc.

Foundation round: 2ch (counts as first dc), work 11dc in ring, join with a ss in 2nd of 2ch. 12 sts.

1st round: 2ch, 1dc in st at base of ch, 2dc in each st to

Abbreviations:
beg = beginning
ch = chain(s)
cm = centimetre(s)
cont = continue
dc = double crochet
dtr2tog = double treble 2 together as foll: all into next st work *y2rh, insert hook in st and draw through a loop, (yrh and draw through 2 loops) twice, rep from * once more, yrh and draw through all 3 loops
foll = follows
patt = pattern
rep = repeat
RS = right side
ss = slip stitch
st(s) = stitch(es)
WS = wrong side
yrh = yarn round hook
y2rh = yarn twice round hook

end, join with a ss in 2nd of 2ch. 24 sts.
2nd round: 2ch, miss st at base of ch, 1dc in each st to end, join with a ss in 2nd of 2ch.

3rd round: 2ch, miss st at base of ch, 2dc in next st, (1dc in next st, 2dc in next st) to end, join with a ss in 2nd of 2ch. 36 sts.

4th round: 2ch, miss st at base of ch, 1dc in next st, 2dc in next st, (1dc in each of next 2 sts, 2dc in next st) to end, join with a ss in 2nd of 2ch. 48 sts.

5th round: As 2nd.

6th round: 2ch, miss st at base of ch, 1dc in each of next 2 sts, 2dc in next st, (1dc in each of next 3 sts, 2dc in next st) to end, join with a ss in 2nd of 2ch. 60 sts.

7th round: 2ch, miss st at base of ch, 1dc in each of next 3 sts,

2dc in next st, (1dc in each of next 4 sts, 2dc in next st) to end, join with a ss in 2nd of 2ch. 72 sts.

8th round: As 2nd.

9th round: 2ch, miss st at base of ch, 1dc in each of next 4 sts, 2dc in next st, (1dc in each of next 5 sts, 2dc in next st) to end, join with a ss in 2nd of 2ch. 84 sts.

10th round: 2ch, miss st at base of ch, 1dc in each of next 5 sts, 2dc in next st, (1dc in each of next 6 sts, 2dc in next st) to end, join with a ss in 2nd of 2ch. 96 sts.

11th round: As 2nd.

12th round: 2ch, miss st at base of ch, 1dc in each of next 6 sts, 2dc in next st, (1dc in each of next 7 sts, 2dc in next st) to end, join with a ss in 2nd of 2ch. 108 sts.

13th round: 2ch, miss st at base of ch, 1dc in each of next 7 sts, 2dc in next st, (1dc in each of next 8 sts, 2dc in next st) to end, join with a ss in 2nd of 2ch. 120 sts.

14th round: As 2nd.

15th round: 2ch, miss st at base of ch, 1dc in each of next 8 sts, 2dc in next st, (1dc in each of next 9 sts, 2dc in next st) to end, join with a ss in 2nd of 2ch. 132 sts.

16th round: 2ch, miss st at base of ch, 1dc in each of next 9 sts, 2dc in next st, (1dc in each of next 10 sts, 2dc in next st) to end, join with a ss in 2nd of 2ch. 144 sts.

17th round: As 2nd. Fasten off, leaving a long tail for sewing up.

BAG MAIN PART:
With 4.50mm (UK 7) hook and two strands of A, make 53ch.

Note: Work each st in **front** loop only of previous sts; start each row with 2ch as indicated to count as first dc.

Foundation row: 1dc in 3rd ch from hook, 1dc in each ch to end, turn. 52 sts.

1st row: 2ch (counts as first dc), miss st at base of ch, 1dc in each st to end, working last dc in 2nd of 2ch and changing to B on last part of last st, turn.

Carry colours not in use loosely along edge – this edge is sewn to base when making up bag.

Always change colour on last part of last st on 2nd row of stripes.

Cont in rows of dc, working 2 rows in B and 2 rows in C, then work 2-row stripes of A, B and C in turn, until work measures 84cm (33in) from beg, ending with 2nd row of a C stripe. Fasten off, leaving a long tail for sewing up.

HANDLES: (make 2)
With 4.50mm (UK 7) hook and two strands of A, make 8ch, join with a ss in first ch to form a ring.

Note: Work each st in **back** loop only of previous sts; start each round with 2ch as indicated to count as first dc.

Foundation round: 2ch (counts as first dc), 1dc in each of next 7ch, join with a ss in 2nd of 2ch. 8 sts.

1st round: 2ch, miss st at base of ch, 1dc in each st to end, join with a ss in 2nd of 2ch. Rep last round until work measures 68cm (27in) from beg. Fasten off.

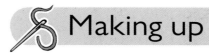

Making up

Oversew two short ends of main part together to form a tube. With WS facing out, oversew main part to base through loops of last round. Turn RS out and sew handles to top edge as shown in photograph.

Felting:
Place bag in a washing machine and wash at 60 degrees with a short spin. Use normal washing powder but do not use conditioner and add a few towels to the machine to provide friction and aid felting process. At end of wash cycle, remove bag and gently squeeze out excess water.

To shape bag, place it over a suitable item (such as a large upturned plastic flowerpot) and leave to dry completely before removing. The drying process can take a few days depending on temperature and humidity.

Finishing:
Flower: (make 6)
With 4.50mm (UK 7) hook and two strands of D, make a magic circle (see Note on page 54), then work 1ch and 10dc in loop, join with a ss to first dc.

1st round: (4ch, dtr2tog in next st, 4ch, 1dc in next st) 5 times omitting last dc, join with a ss in base of 4ch. Fasten off, leaving a long tail.

Arrange flowers in a cluster, evenly spaced, on front of bag and sew in place using long tails of yarn. Using tapestry needle threaded with two strands of E, stitch stems as foll: secure end of yarn in centre of a flower (this will be covered later by button) and bring needle up through bag fabric at top of stem. Insert needle back through fabric at base of stem to create a single line of yarn. Bring needle to front again about 2mm (1/8in) up from base of stem and adjacent to it, then take it over strand of yarn and back through to form small neat st that holds long strand in place. Rep at intervals of less than 4mm (1/4in) up length of stem, then bring yarn back up through centre of flower and fasten off. Rep to make stems for other five flowers.

Sew on buttons to centre of flowers.

Trilby hatbands

Customise your hat with a choice of two bands, which you can crochet in an afternoon.

Trim a plain hat with a choice of colourful crochet bands that feature eye-catching motifs – either a pretty double-layered flower motif with a sparkling diamante at its centre or a graphic line-up of **X** motifs.

The Yarn

Anchor Style Creativa Fino (approx. 125m/ 136 yards per 50g/ 1¾oz ball) is 100% mercerized cotton in a 4-ply weight, ideal for craft projects. There is a wide range of shades.

GETTING STARTED

All elements of these hatbands are easy to work.

Striped band:
Approximately 66cm (26in) long x 2cm (¾in) wide

Hugs & kisses band:
Approximately 66cm (26in) long x 2.5cm (¾in) wide

How much yarn:
Striped band: 1 x 50g (1¾oz) ball of Anchor Style Creativa Fino in each of four colours: A – Apple Green (shade 01330); B – Grey (shade 00235); C – Dark Purple (shade 01309) and D – Orange (shade 01338)

Hugs & kisses band: 1 x 50g (1¾oz) ball of Anchor Style Creativa Fino in each of three colours: A – Dark Pink (shade 01320); B – Light Pink (shade 01317) and C – Red (shade 01333)

Hook:
2.50mm (UK 12) crochet hook

Additional items:
Diamante bead for Striped band
Sewing needle and purple thread for Striped band
Stick-on Velcro dots (optional)

Tension:
Striped band: 22 sts measure 10cm (4in) over tr on 2.50mm (UK 12) hook

Hugs & kisses band: Circular motifs measure 1.5cm (⅝in) in diameter after 1st round on 2.50mm (UK 12) hook

What you have to do:
Striped band:
Work a long strip of double foundation chain in one colour. Work along other side of strip adding a row of trebles in a second colour. Make a double layered flower motif with leaf. Sew on stick-on Velcro dots as a fastener if required.

Hugs & kisses band:
Work a series of simple circular motifs in double crochet. Join motifs together into a band with another round of double crochet. Work three X motifs and sew on to band. Use stick-on Velcro dots as a fastener if required.

Instructions

Abbreviations:

beg = beginning
ch = chain(s)
cm = centimetre(s)
dc = double crochet
foll = follows
htr = half treble
rep = repeat
RS = right side
sp = space
ss = slip stitch
st(s) = stitch(es)
tr = treble
yrh = yarn round hook

Note: To make a Magic Circle, wrap yarn clockwise around forefinger twice to form a ring. Holding end of yarn between thumb and middle finger, insert hook into ring and draw yarn from ball through.

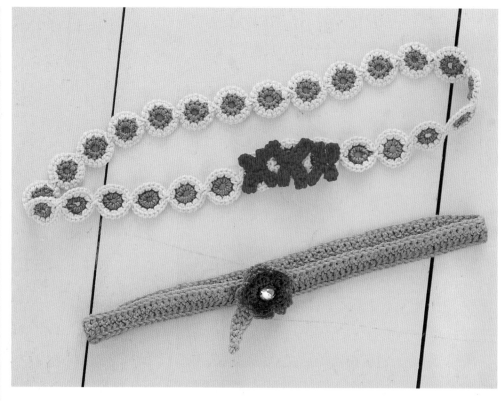

STRIPED BAND WITH FLOWER:

With 2.50mm (UK 12) hook and A, make 3ch and work a double foundation ch as foll:

1st row: (RS) Yrh, insert hook into first ch, yrh and draw through a loop (3 loops on hook), yrh and draw through first loop on hook to create one ch st (this creates base ch through which 2nd row of tr in B are worked), (yrh and draw through first two loops on hook) twice to complete tr (2 sts), *yrh, insert hook into ch made at beg of last st, yrh and draw through a loop (3 loops on hook), yrh and draw through first loop on hook to create one ch st, (yrh and draw through first two loops on hook) twice, rep from * until work measures approximately 66cm (26in) or required length from beg, work 1ch and fasten off.

2nd row: Turn strip just worked upside down and with RS facing work into base ch, join B into first ch, 3ch, miss st at base of ch, 1tr into each st to end. Fasten off.

Flower motif, first flower:

Make a magic circle (see Note) with C and using 2.50mm (UK 12) hook, cont as foll:

1st round: 1ch (does not count as a st), work 5dc into ring, join with a ss into first dc. 5 sts.

2nd round: 1ch, 2dc into each st to end, join with a ss into first dc. 10 sts.

3rd round: *3tr and 1htr into next st, ss into next st, rep from * to end.
5 petals. ** Fasten off, leaving a long end.

Flower motif, second flower:

Using D, work as given for First flower to **.

4th round: Ss into sp between petals, *4ch, ss into top of petal, 4ch, ss into sp between petals, rep from * all round. Fasten off, leaving a long end.

Leaf:

With 2.50mm (UK 12) hook and A, make 2ch. Work a double foundation ch as given for Striped band until there are 10 sts, turn and work back along base of ch as foll: 1ch, 1tr into each of next 4 sts, 1htr into next st, 1dc into each of next 2 sts, ss into each of next 3 sts. Fasten off, leaving a long end.

HUGS & KISSES BAND:
Circular motif: (make 27)
With 2.50mm (UK 12) hook and A, make 5ch, join with a ss into first ch to form a ring.

1st round: 1ch (does not count as a st), work 10dc into ring, join with a ss into first dc. Fasten off and weave in tail.

Band:
With 2.50mm (UK 12) hook, join B into any st of first circular motif, 1ch, then work 2dc into each of next 5 sts (10 sts), *insert hook into any st of next circular motif, 2dc into same st, 2dc into each of next 4 sts (10 sts), rep from * until all circular motifs have been joined into a band. On last circular motif, cont working 2dc into each st until motif is completely encircled, join with a ss into first dc. **Remove hook from loop, insert hook into next unworked st on adjacent circular motif and draw loop through, cont working 2dc into each st until motif is completely encircled, join with a ss into first dc, rep from ** to end.

Fastening tab:
1st row: 1ch (does not count as a st), 1dc into each of next 2 sts, turn.

2nd row: 1ch, 1dc into each of first 2dc, 1htr into each of next 2dc, turn.

3rd–5th rows: 1ch, 1dc into each of next 4 sts, turn. Fasten off.

Large X motif:
With 2.50mm (UK 12) hook and C, make 9ch.

Foundation row: Insert hook into 2nd ch from hook, *yrh and draw a loop through, yrh and draw through first loop on hook, yrh and draw through both loops on hook, insert hook into next ch and rep from * to end of row, turn. 8 sts.

Next row: 1ch, ss into each of first 4 sts, make 6ch, *1htr into 3rd ch from hook, 1htr into each of next 3ch, ss into st at base of ch *, make another 6ch, rep from * to *, ss into each of next 4 sts. Fasten off.

Small X motif: (make 2)
With 2.50mm (UK 12) hook and C, make 7ch. Work foundation row as given for Large motif. 6 sts.

Next row: 1ch, ss into each of first 3 sts, make 5ch, *1htr into 3rd ch from hook, 1htr into each of next 2ch, ss into st at base of ch *, make another 5ch, rep from * to *, ss into each of next 3 sts.
Fasten off, leaving a long tail.

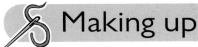 Making up

STRIPED BAND WITH FLOWER:
Sew diamante bead to centre of first flower. Place first flower centrally on top of second flower and sew in place. Sew wider end of leaf to back of double-layer flower and sew flower in place on one end of hatband. If required, attach stick-on Velcro dots to each end of hatband to create a fastening.

HUGS & KISSES BAND:
Position small X motifs either side of large one and use long tails to sew together, joining their adjacent 'legs' as shown in the photograph. Positioning large X motif over last circular motif on end without tab, sew X motifs securely in place to band. If required, attach stick-on Velcro dots to tab and underside of first circular motif to create a fastening.

Bolero with flower motifs

This little bolero is the perfect cover-up over a dress or top.

Made in a simple but pretty openwork pattern, this bolero has shaped front edges trimmed at the neckline with a corsage consisting of flower motifs and leaves.

GETTING STARTED

Pattern is easy to follow; motifs should be sewn on neatly for a professional finish.

Size:
To fit bust: 86[91:97:102]cm (34[36:38:40]in)
Actual size: 91[97:102.5:108.5]cm (36[38:40½:42¾]in)
Length: 37.5[39:41:42.5]cm (14¾[15½:16:16¾]in)
Sleeve seam: 30cm (12in)
Note: Figures in square brackets [ ] refer to larger sizes; where there is only one set of figures, it applies to all sizes

How much yarn:
10[10:11:11] x 50g (1¾oz) balls of Rico Essentials Merino DK in Mulberry (shade 19)

Hook:
4.00mm (UK 8) crochet hook

Tension:
21 sts (7 clusters) and 13 rows measure 10cm (4in) square over patt on 4.00mm (UK 8) hook
IT IS ESSENTIAL TO WORK TO THE STATED TENSION TO ACHIEVE SUCCESS

What you have to do:
Work in pattern as described with clusters of double crochet, half treble and treble worked into same stitch. Shape front edges, armholes and neckline as instructed. Make individual small and large flower motifs in the round, plus leaves. Sew floral motifs to each side of front neckline.

The Yarn
Rico Essentials Merino DK (approx. 120m/131 yards per 50g/1¾oz ball) contains 100% merino wool in a superwash format. It is a classic wool yarn in plenty of mouthwatering colours.

Instructions

Abbreviations:

beg = beginning
ch = chain(s)
cl(s) = cluster(s) formed
by working (1dc, 1htr
and 1tr) in same place
cm = centimetre(s)
cont = continue
dc = double crochet
dec = decrease(d)
dtr = double treble
foll = following
htr = half treble
inc = increase(d)
patt = pattern
rem = remain(ing)
rep = repeat
sp = space
ss = slip stitch
st(s) = stitch(es)
tr = treble

LEFT FRONT:

With 4.00mm (UK 8) hook make
24[27:30:33]ch.

Foundation row: (1htr, 1tr) into 3rd ch
from hook, *miss 2ch, (1dc, 1htr, 1tr) into
next ch, rep from * to last 3ch, miss 2ch,
1dc into last ch, turn.

Patt row: 1ch (counts as first dc), (1htr,

1tr) into st at base of first ch, *miss (1tr,
1htr), (1dc, 1htr, 1tr) into next dc, rep
from * to last 3 sts, miss (1tr, 1htr), 1dc
into turning ch, turn. 22[25:28:31] sts;
7[8:9:10] cls.

Shape front edge:

Inc row: Patt to last cl, (1dc, 1htr, 1tr)
into turning ch, turn. 1 cl inc.
Patt 3 rows straight. Rep last 4 rows until
there are 40[43:46:49] sts; 13[14:15:16]
cls, then patt 2 rows straight, ending at
shaped edge (work should measure 20cm
(8in) from beg).

Shape armhole:

Next row: Patt to last 2 cls, turn.
34[37:40:43] sts; 11[12:13:14] cls.
Keeping armhole edge straight, cont to inc
at front edge as before on next and foll
4th row. 40[43:46:49] sts; 13[14:15:16] cls.
Work straight until armhole measures
10[10:12:12]cm (4[4:4¾:4¾]in) from beg,
ending at armhole edge.

Shape front:

Dec row: Patt to last cl, turn. 3 sts;
1 cl dec.
Patt 1 row straight. Rep last 2 rows until
25[25:28:28] sts; 8[8:9:9] cls rem, ending
at armhole edge.
Fasten off.

RIGHT FRONT:

Work as given for Left front.

BACK:

With 4.00mm (UK 8) hook make 99[105:111:117]ch. Work foundation row and patt row as given for Left front. 97[103:109:115] sts; 32[34:36:38] cls.
Rep last row to form patt until Back measures same as Left front to armhole.

Shape armholes:

Next 2 rows: Patt to last 2 cls, turn. 85[91:97:103] sts; 28[30:32:34] cls.
Cont in patt without shaping until Back measures same as Left front. Fasten off.

SLEEVES: (make 2)

With 4.00mm (UK 8) hook make 66[69:72:75]ch. Work foundation row and patt row as given for Left front. 64[67:70:73] sts; 21[22:23:24] cls. Rep last row to form patt until Sleeve measures 30cm (12in) from beg.

Shape top:

Next 2 rows: Patt to last 2 cls, turn. 52[55:58:61] sts; 17[18:19:20] cls.
Next row: Patt to last cl, turn. 3 sts; 1 cl dec.
Rep last row until 22 sts; 7 cls rem. Fasten off.

SMALL FLOWER: (make 4)

With 4.00mm (UK 8) hook make 5ch, join with a ss into first ch to form a ring.
1st round: 1ch, work 10dc into ring, join with a ss into first ch.
2nd round: 1ch, *miss next dc, (1dc, 1htr, 1tr, 1htr, 1dc) into next dc, rep from * 4 times more, join with a ss into first dc worked. Fasten off.

LARGE FLOWER: (make 2)

With 4.00mm (UK 8) hook make 5ch, join with a ss into first ch to form a ring.
1st round: 1ch, work 15dc into ring, join with a ss into first dc.
2nd round: 4ch, miss dc at base of ch and foll 2dc, ss into next dc, *4ch, miss next 2dc, ss into next dc, rep from * twice more, 4ch, miss last 2dc, join with a ss into first of 4ch.
3rd round: 1ch (counts as first dc), work (4htr, 1tr, 4htr, 1dc into first ch sp, *(1dc, 4htr, 1tr, 4htr, 1dc) into next ch sp, rep from * 3 times more, join with a ss into first ch. Fasten off.

LEAVES: (make 4)

With 4.00mm (UK 8) hook make 15ch.
1st row: 1dc into 2nd ch from hook, *1htr into next ch, 1tr into each of next 3ch, 1dtr into each of next 4ch, 1tr into each of next 3ch, 1htr into next ch *, (1dc, 3ch, 1dc) into last ch, now work back along other side of foundation ch, rep from * to *, 1dc into last ch. Fasten off.

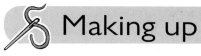

Making up

Join shoulder seams. Sew in sleeves, then join side and sleeve seams. Pin leaves and flowers in place along neckline as shown in photograph and sew firmly in place with small, neat stitches.

Embossed scarf

Embellish the ends of a plain scarf with a collection of crochet motifs to great effect.

Worked in a luxurious and soft yarn, this scarf has a panel at each end decorated with a sewn-on arrangement of shapes to give an attractive embossed effect.

GETTING STARTED

★ *Scarf is worked in an easy stitch pattern and decorated with simple shapes.*

Size:
Finished scarf measures 21 x 137cm (8½ x 54in)

How much yarn:
6 x 50g (1¾oz) balls of Sublime Cashmere Merino Silk Aran in Bay (shade 135)

Hook:
4.50mm (UK 7) crochet hook

Tension:
21 sts and 10 rows measure 11cm (4¼in) square over patt on 4.50mm (UK 7) hook
IT IS ESSENTIAL TO WORK TO THE STATED TENSION TO ACHIEVE SUCCESS

What you have to do:
Work panel at each end of scarf in trebles. Work main pattern with pairs of trebles separated by a chain space. Make selection of simple shapes, mainly in the round, to sew on to create an embossed effect.

The Yarn
Sublime Cashmere Merino Silk Aran (approx. 86m/94 yards per 50g/1¾oz ball) is a blend of 75% merino wool, 20% silk and 5% cashmere. It produces a very soft, luxurious fabric that can be hand-washed. The large colour palette includes subtle pastels and strong shades.

Instructions

Abbreviations:

beg = beginning
ch = chain
cm = centimetre(s)
cont = continue
dc = double crochet
foll = follow(s)(ing)
htr = half treble
patt = pattern
rep = repeat
RS = right side
sp = space
ss = slip stitch
st(s) = stitch(es)
tr = treble
tr2tog = work 1tr into each of next 2 sts leaving last loop of each on hook, yarn round hook and draw through all 3 loops
yrh = yarn round hook

SCARF

With 4.50mm (UK 7) hook make 43ch.

Foundation row: (RS) 1tr into 4th ch from hook, 1tr into each ch to end, turn. 41 sts.

1st row: 3ch (counts as first tr), miss st at base of ch, 1tr into each st to end, working last tr into 3rd of 3ch, turn. Work 11 more rows in tr, then cont in patt as foll:

Next row: 3ch, miss st at base of ch and foll st, (1tr, 1ch, 1tr) into next st, *miss next 2 sts, (1tr, 1ch, 1tr) into next st, rep from * 11 times more, miss next st, 1tr into 3rd of 3ch, turn.

Next row: 3ch, *(1tr, 1ch, 1tr) into ch sp between next 2tr, rep from * 12 times more, 1tr into 3rd of 3ch, turn. Rep last row to form patt until work measures 122cm (48in) from beg.

Next row: 3ch, miss st at base of ch, 1tr into each tr and 1tr into each ch sp to end, turn. 41 sts. Work 12 more rows in tr. Fasten off.

SPIRAL FLOWER: (make 7)

With 4.50mm (UK 7) hook make 21ch.

1st row: 1dc into 2nd ch from hook, 1htr into next ch, 2tr into each ch to end. Fasten off leaving a 30cm (12in) tail of yarn.

Thread yarn tail into a tapestry needle. Coil length of crochet into a flat circle, starting at beg of row. Slip stitch bottom edge to back of trebles as you work. Secure yarn and leave a long end for stitching to scarf.

Vary number of starting ch between 21 and 32 to give flowers of different sizes.

DOME 1: (make 3)

With 4.50mm (UK 7) hook make 3ch, join with a ss into first ch to form a ring.

1st round: 1ch, work 11dc into ring, join with a ss into first ch.

2nd round: 1ch, 2dc into each dc to end, join with a ss into first ch.

3rd round: 2ch, (tr2tog) to end, ss into 2nd of 2ch. Fasten off, leaving long end for stitching to scarf.

On one dome work 1 round of dc before working final round.

DOME 2: (make 6)

With 4.50mm (UK 7) hook make 5ch, join with a ss into first ch to form a ring.

1st round: 3ch, work 15tr into ring, join with a ss into 3rd of 3ch.

2nd round: 1ch, 1dc into each st, join with a ss into first ch.

3rd round: As 2nd.

Fasten off, leaving a long end for stitching to scarf.

Vary number of sts on 1st round between 15 and 19.

FLUTED FLOWER 1: (make 6)

With 4.50mm (UK 7) hook make 5ch, join with a ss into first ch to form a ring.

1st round: 1ch, work 14dc into ring, join with a ss into first ch.

2nd round: 1ch, 2dc into each st to end, join with a ss into first ch.

Rep last round twice more. Fasten off, leaving a long end for stitching to scarf.

Work 4 flowers as given. For 5th flower substitute htr for dc on 2nd–4th rounds. Work 6th flower as 5th but fasten off after 3rd round.

FLUTED FLOWER 2: (make 3)

With 4.50mm (UK 7) hook make 3ch, join with a ss into first ch.

1st round: 3ch, work 15tr into ring, join with a ss into 3rd of 3ch.

2nd round: 1ch, 2dc into each st to end, join with a ss into first ch.

Rep last round 2 or 3 times. Fasten off, leaving a long end for stitching to scarf.

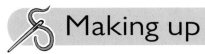 Making up

Arrange embossed shapes across solid panels at each end of scarf, moving them around until you have a well-spaced arrangement. Pin in place, then sew down using the long end of yarn attached. Slip stitch around edges of domes and spirals, and catch down outer edge of fluted flowers at intervals to create a petalled effect.

Floral hairband

Scatter these pretty flowers and leaves over a hairband to achieve a sweetly old-fashioned look.

Cover a bought fabric-covered hairband with a meadow of flower motifs worked in delicate embroidery thread in pretty colours, including plain and variegated shades.

The Yarn

Traditionally used for embroidery, DMC Pearl and Colour Variations Pearl are non-divisible cotton threads with a silky sheen and satin feel that are perfect for other crafting projects, such as small crochet items. The Colour Variations Pearl thread contains a multitude of tonal shades to create interesting effects without swapping the thread.

GETTING STARTED

 Very simple motifs but worked with fine embroidery thread.

Size:

Hairband to fit an adult head

Small flower is approximately 1.5cm (⅝in) in diameter; large flower is approximately 3cm (⅝in) in diameter

How much yarn:

1 x 25m (27 yard) skein of DMC Pearl art.115 size 5 in each of three colours: A – Pale Green (shade 472); B – Bright Pink (shade 600) and C – Lime Green (shade 907)

1 x 25m (27 yard) skein of DMC Colour Variations Pearl size 5 in each of seven colours: D – Turquoise (shade 4045); E – Lime Green (shade 4050); F – Cream/Lemon (shade 4077); G – Orange (shade 4124); H – Pink/Orange (shade 4190);

I – Fuchsia/Red (shade 4200) and J – Blue/Mauve (shade 4215)

Hook:

2.50mm (UK 12) crochet hook

Additional items:

Hairband, 3.5cm (1⅜in) at widest point, covered in black jersey fabric

Sewing needle and thread

What you have to do:

Make a selection of large and small floral motifs and leaves. Use simple stitches and plain or combination of variegated shades as described. Sew flowers on to a bought hairband.

Instructions

Abbreviations:

ch = chain(s)
cm = centimetre(s)
cont = continue
dc = double crochet
foll = follows
htr = half treble
ss = slip stitch
tr = treble

SMALL FLOWER: (make 13)
With 2.50mm (UK 12) hook, make a magic circle (see Note on page 54), 1ch (counts as first dc), work 5dc into ring, pull up tightly and change to petal colour (if required) before joining with a ss into first ch.
2nd round: (2ch, ss into next dc) 6 times. Fasten off.
Make 13 Small flowers in total in colours as foll:
1 each in H and J and 2 in F
1 with centre in F and petals in J
2 with centre in A and petals in B
2 with centre in F and petals in G
2 with centre in A and petals in H
2 with centre in C and petals in I

LARGE FLOWER: (make 3)
With 2.50mm (UK 12) hook, make a magic circle, 1ch (counts as first dc), work 5dc into ring, pull up tightly and

change to petal colour before joining with a ss into first ch.

2nd round: (2ch, ss into next dc) 6 times.

3rd round: Into each ch sp work
(1dc, 3tr and 1dc) to form 6 petals. Fasten off.

Make 3 Large flowers in total in colours as foll:

1 with centre in A and petals in B

1 with centre in C and petals in I

1 with centre in F and petals in G

SMALL LEAF: (make 6)

With 2.50mm (UK 12) hook make 5ch.

1st row: Ss into 2nd ch from hook, 1dc into next ch, 1htr into next ch, 1dc into last ch. Fasten off.

Make 6 Small leaves in total in colours as foll:

1 each in D and E

2 each in A and C

LARGE LEAF: (make 6)

With 2.50mm (UK 12) hook make 8ch.

1st row: 1dc into 3rd ch from hook, 1htr into next ch, 1tr into next ch, 1htr into next ch, 1dc into next ch, 3dc into last ch, then cont along other side of foundation ch, working 1dc into next ch, 1htr into next ch, 1tr into next ch, 1htr into next ch, 1dc into next ch, ss into next ch. Fasten off.

Make 6 Large leaves in total in colours as foll:

1 each in C and E

2 each in A and D

Making up

Starting at widest point at top of hairband, sew large flowers and leaves in position, stitching through fabric on hairband. Then position small flowers and leaves down each side of hairband and sew to hairband fabric once you are happy with their placement and colour balance.

Funky flower mats

Give your dining table a retro look with these cheery flower-shaped mats in different sizes.

These bright and cheerful flower-shaped table mats are worked in a cotton yarn and can have a plain or patterned reverse side for heatproof protection. You can also include a layer of wadding, if required, for extra padding.

The Yarn

Rowan Cotton Glacé (approx. 115m/125 yards per 50g/1¾oz ball) is 100% cotton. It has a good matt finish and can be machine washed. There are many colours.

GETTING STARTED

 Straightforward to work but there are a lot of colour changes.

Size:

Large mat: *approximately 30cm (12in) in diameter*

Small mat: *approximately 16cm (6¼in) in diameter*

How much yarn:

2 x 50g (1¾oz) balls of Rowan Cotton Glace in colour A – Blood Orange (shade 445)
1 ball in each of four other colours: B – Ochre (shade 833); C – Persimmon (shade 832); D – Bubbles (shade 724); E – Shoot (shade 814)

Hook:

3.00mm (UK 11) crochet hook

Additional item:

Wadding (optional)

Tension:

20 sts and 10 rows measure 10cm (4in) square over tr on 3.00mm (UK 11) hook
IT IS ESSENTIAL TO WORK TO THE STATED TENSION TO ACHIEVE SUCCESS

What you have to do:

Work centre of mats in rounds of trebles and double crochet using colours as described. Work individual petals in rows and stripes and then crochet petals onto centre of mat to form a flower shape. Work back of mats in same way using a plain colour or same colours as front. Crochet front and back together, inserting wadding for extra thickness if required.

Instructions

Abbreviations:

ch = chain(s)
cm = centimetre(s)
cont = continue
dc = double crochet
foll = follows
htr = half treble
rep = repeat
ss = slip stitch
st(s) = stitch(es)
tog = together
tr = treble
yrh = yarn round hook

LARGE MAT:
Front: With 3.00mm (UK 11) hook and B, make 6ch, join with a ss in first ch to form a ring.

1st round: 3ch (counts as first tr), work 11tr in ring, join with a ss in 3rd of 3ch. 12 sts.

2nd round: 3ch, 1tr in st at base of ch, *2tr in next st, rep from * to end, join with a ss in 3rd of 3ch. 24 sts.

3rd round: 3ch, 1tr in st at base of ch, 1tr in next st, *2tr in next st, 1tr in next st, rep from * to end, changing to A on last st, join with a ss in 3rd of 3ch. 36 sts.

4th round: With A, 1ch (does not count as a st), miss st at base of ch, *2dc in next st, 1dc in next st, rep from * to end, working last dc in st at base of ch and changing to C on last st, join with a ss in first dc. 54 sts.

5th round: With C, 3ch, miss st at base of ch, 1tr in next st, 2tr in next st, *1tr in each of next 2 sts, 2tr in next st, rep from * to end, changing to D on last st, join with a ss in 3rd of 3ch. 72 sts.

6th round: With D, 3ch, 1tr in st at base of ch, 1tr in each of next 3 sts, *2tr in next st, 1tr in each of next 3 sts, rep from * to end, join with a ss in 3rd of 3ch. 90 sts.

7th round: 3ch, 1tr in st at base of ch, 1tr in each of next 5 sts, *2tr in next st, 1tr in each of next 5 sts, rep from * to end, join with a ss in 3rd of 3ch. 105 sts.

8th round: 3ch, miss st at base of ch, 1tr in each st to end, changing to C on last st, join with a ss in 3rd of 3ch.

9th round: With C, 1ch, 1dc in each st to end, join with a ss in first dc. Fasten off. 105 sts.

Petals: (make 7)

With 3.00mm (UK 11) hook and C, make 6ch, join with a ss in first ch to form a ring.

1st row: 3ch (counts as first tr), work 9tr in ring, turn. 10 sts.

2nd row: 3ch, 1tr in st at base of ch, 2tr in each st to end, omitting turning ch, turn. 18 sts.

3rd row: 3ch, 1tr in st at base of ch, *1tr in next st, 2tr in next st, rep from * to end, changing to D on last st and omitting turning ch, turn. 26 sts.

4th row: With D, 1ch (does not count as a st), 2dc in st at base of ch, *1dc in each of next 4 sts, 2dc in next st, rep from * to end, working last st in 3rd of 3ch. 32 sts. Fasten off.

Join petals to mat:

1st joining round: With A, insert hook in any st on 9th round of mat and work 1dc in same st, cont around outer edge of petal as foll: *1dc in each of next 5 sts, (2dc in next st, 1dc in each of next 3 sts) twice, 2dc in next st, 1dc in each of next 4 sts, (2dc in next st, 1dc in each of next 3 sts) twice, 2dc in next st, 1dc in each of next 5 sts, miss 13 sts around outer edge of mat, 1dc in each of next 2 sts on mat, then rep from * until all petals have been attached, omitting 1dc at end of last rep. Fasten off.

Sew row-ends of each petal to corresponding 13 free sts of 9th round (between pairs of dc of 1st joining round).

2nd joining round: Miss first 4 sts of last round, join E to next st, work 1dc in same st, *1dc in each of next 5 sts, 1htr in each of next 2 sts, 1tr in each of next 16 sts, 1htr in each of next 2 sts, 1dc in each of next 6 sts, insert hook in next st, yrh and draw through a loop, miss next 6 sts, insert hook in next st, yrh and draw through a loop, yrh and draw through all 3 loops on hook, 1dc in next st, rep from * omitting 1dc at end of last rep. Fasten off. If using wadding, use mat as a template and cut out wadding to same shape.

Back:

Work as given for Front, using A throughout until 1st joining round has been completed, then work 2nd joining round with E but do not fasten off.

SMALL MAT:
Back:

Work as given for Large mat front until 4th round has been completed, using B for 1st and 2nd rounds, C for 3rd round and A for 4th round. 54 sts. Do not fasten off at end of 4th round, leave st on a holder and yarn attached.

Petals: (make 6)

With 3.00mm (UK 11) hook and D, make 4ch, join with a ss in first ch to form a ring. Work 1st and 2nd rows as given for Large mat petals. 18 sts. Fasten off.

Join petals to mat:

1st joining round: Slip st from holder back on hook and with A, 1ch (does not count as a st), 1dc in st at base of ch, cont around outer edge of petal as foll: *1dc in each of next 3 sts, (2dc in next st, 1dc in each of next 4 sts) 3 times, miss 8 sts around outer edge of mat, 1dc in next st on mat, then rep from * until all petals have been attached, omitting 1dc at end of last rep, join with a ss in first dc. Fasten off.

Sew row-ends of each petal to corresponding 8 free sts of 4th round (between single dc of 1st joining round).

2nd joining round: Join E to 5th st of last round, 1ch, 1dc in st at base of ch, *1dc in next st, 2dc in next st, 1dc in each of next 2 sts, 2dc in next st, 1dc in each of next 3 sts, (2dc in next st, 1dc in each of next 2 sts) twice, insert hook in next st, yrh and draw through a loop, miss next 5 sts, insert hook in next st, yrh and draw through a loop, yrh and draw through all 3 loops on hook, 1dc in next st, rep from * omitting 1dc at end of last rep. Fasten off. If using wadding, use mat as a template and cut out wadding to same shape.

Back:

Work as given for Front but do not fasten off E at end of 2nd joining round.

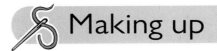 Making up

LARGE MAT:

With E still attached and front of mat facing (and wadding inserted between the two pieces, if using), work in dc around outer edge of both pieces simultaneously to join.

SMALL MAT:

With E still attached and front of mat facing (and wadding inserted between the two pieces, if using), work in dc around outer edge of both pieces simultaneously to join.

Floral appliqué vest

A sprinkling of spring flowers makes this vest a visual treat.

This neat vest is worked in a luxurious summer yarn and simple stitch pattern. Its neckline has an eye-catching arrangement of flower motifs and leaves that have been sewn on.

GETTING STARTED

⭐⭐ *Easy stitch pattern and shaping for vest, but care is needed with making and sewing on appliqué flowers.*

Size:
To fit bust: *86[92:97:102]cm (34[36:38:40]in)*
Length: *56[58:60:62]cm (22[23:23½:24½]in)*
Note: *Figures in square brackets [ ] refer to larger sizes; where there is only one set of figures, it applies to all sizes*

How much yarn:
8[8:9:9] x 50g (1¾oz) balls of Debbie Bliss Amalfi in colour A – Green (shade 18)
1 ball in each of three other colours: B – Yellow (shade 07); C – Pale Pink (shade 01) and D – Pink (shade 02)

Hooks:
3.50mm (UK 9) crochet hook
4.00mm (UK 8) crochet hook

Tension:
21 sts and 20 rows measure 10cm (4in) square over patt on 4.00mm (UK 8) hook
IT IS ESSENTIAL TO WORK TO THE STATED TENSION TO ACHIEVE SUCCESS

What you have to do:
Work back and front in a simple double crochet and chain pattern. Shape armholes and neck as directed. Work double crochet edging around all edges. Crochet flowers and leaves and sew around front neckline.

The Yarn
Debbie Bliss Amalfi (approx. 100m/109 yards per 50g/1¾oz ball) contains 70% cotton, 15% viscose, 10% linen and 5% silk. It is a double-knitting weight yarn in a luxurious blend of fibres. The yarn is machine washable at a low temperature and there is a comprehensive shade palette of delicious ice-cream colours.

Instructions

BACK:
With 4.00mm (UK 8) hook and A, make 90[96:102:106]ch.
Foundation row: (RS) 1dc into 4th ch from hook, *1ch, miss next ch, 1dc into next ch, rep from * to end, turn.

89[95:101:105] sts.
1st row: 1ch (counts as first st), 1dc into next ch sp, *1ch, 1dc into next ch sp, rep from * to end, 1dc into next ch, turn.
2nd row: 2ch (counts as 1dc and 1ch), 1dc into next ch

Abbreviations:

beg = beginning
ch = chain
cm = centimetre(s)
cont = continue
dc = double crochet
dec = decrease
dec 2 sts = insert hook into next ch sp, yrh and draw a loop through, yrh, insert hook into next ch sp, yrh and draw a loop through, yrh and draw through first two loops on hook, yrh and draw through all 3 loops
dtr = double treble
htr = half treble
patt = pattern
rem = remaining
rep = repeat
RS = right side
sp = space
ss = slip stitch
st(s) = stitch(es)
tr = treble
WS = wrong side
yrh = yarn round hook

sp, *1ch, 1dc into next ch sp, rep from *, ending with 1ch, 1dc into 1ch, turn. The last 2 rows form patt. Rep them until work measures 37[38:40:41]cm (14½[15:15¾:16]in) from beg, ending with a WS row.

Shape armholes:

1st row: (RS) Ss into each of first 4[6:4:4] sts, 2ch (does not count as a st), miss first dc, 1dc into next ch sp, (1ch, 1dc into next ch sp) 37[38:43:45] times, 1ch, dec 2 sts, turn. 77[79:89:93] sts.

2nd row: As 1st patt row, noting last st is worked into last dc of previous row and not 2ch, which form dec at this edge.

3rd row: 2ch, 1dc into next ch sp, patt to last 3 sts, dec 2 sts, turn. 73[75:85:89] sts. Rep last 2 rows to dec 2 sts at each end of every RS row 4[4:6:6] times more.

57[59:61:65] sts.**

Work straight in patt until armholes measure 17[18:18:19]cm (6¾[7:7:7½]in) from beg, ending with a WS row.

Shape back neck:

Next row: (RS) Patt 12[12:14:14] sts, dec 2 sts, turn and complete this side of neck first.

Next row: Patt to end, turn.

Next row: Patt to last 3 sts, dec 2 sts, turn. 11[11:13:13] sts.

Next row: Patt to end. Fasten off.
With RS facing, miss centre 27[29:27:31] sts at base of neck, rejoin yarn in next ch sp, 2ch (does not count as a st), miss first dc, 1dc into next ch sp, patt to end, turn.

Next row: Patt to end, turn.

Next row: 2ch (does not count as a st), miss first dc, 1dc into next ch sp, patt to end, turn. 11[11:13:13] sts.

Next row: Patt to end. Fasten off.

FRONT:

Work as given for Back to **.
Work straight in patt until armholes measure 8[9:9:10]cm (3¼[3½:3½:4]in)

from beg, ending with a WS row.

Shape neck:

Next row: (RS) Patt 20[20:22:22] sts, dec 2 sts, turn and complete this side of neck first.

Next row: Patt to end, turn.

Next row: Patt to last 3 sts, dec 2 sts, turn.

Rep last 2 rows 4 times more. 11[11:13:13] sts. Work straight until armhole matches Back to shoulder, ending with a WS row. Fasten off.

With RS facing, miss centre 11[13:11:15] sts at base of neck, rejoin yarn in next ch sp, 2ch (does not count as a st), miss first dc, 1dc into next ch sp, patt to end, turn.

Next row: Patt to end, turn.

Next row: 2ch (does not count as a st), miss first dc, 1dc into next ch sp, patt to end, turn.

Rep last 2 rows 4 times more. 11[11:13:13] sts. Work straight until armhole matches Back to shoulder, ending with a WS row. Fasten off.

LARGE FLOWER: (make 3)

With 3.50mm (UK 9) hook, make a magic circle (see Note on page 54) completing as foll:

1st round: 3ch (counts as first tr), then work 11tr into ring, pull end to close ring, ** using C, join with a ss in 3rd of 3ch. Cut off B. Cont with C.

2nd round: 4ch, (ss into front strand of next tr, 3ch) 11 times, join with a ss into 1st of 4ch. Fasten off.

3rd round: (RS) Working behind sts of 2nd round, join D into back strand of first tr of 1st round, 5ch, (ss into back strand of next tr, 4ch) 11 times, join with a ss into 1st of 5ch. Fasten off.

Variation: (make 1)

Work as given for Large flower to **, then cont as Large flower but substituting D for C and in 3rd round C for D.

SMALL FLOWER: (make 7)

With 3.50mm (UK 9) hook and C, make 6ch, join with a ss into first ch to form a ring.

1st round: (RS) (2ch, 2tr, 2ch, ss into ring) 4 times. Fasten off.

2nd round: (RS) Join B between petals, (1dc between petals and into ring, 1ch behind petal) 4 times, join with a ss into first dc. Fasten off.

Variation: (make 5)

Work as given for Small flower but substituting D for C.

LEAF: (make 4)

With 3.50mm (UK 9) hook and B, make 11ch, **miss

2ch, 1htr into next ch, 1tr into next ch, 1dtr into next ch, 1tr into next ch, 1dc into next ch***, make 7ch, rep from ** to ***, make 7ch, rep from ** to *** again, ss into each of rem 4ch. Fasten off.

Making up

Press front and back according to directions on ball band. Join shoulder and side seams.

Edgings:

With 3.50mm (UK 9) hook and RS facing, join A to side seam at lower edge. Working in remaining strand of foundation ch, work 1dc into each st around lower edge, join with a ss into first dc. Fasten off.

Working into two strands each time, work edging around armholes and neck in this way, missing sts as necessary to maintain a smooth edge.

Appliqué:

Press leaves and outer petals of large flowers. Using photograph as a guide, position flowers randomly around neckline. Use A split into two threads to stitch arrangement in place with long backstitches on WS of work.

Rose cushion

A scattering of roses adorn this stylish cushion, and there are more surprises on the back.

This stunning long cushion has colourful rose motifs sewn onto a natural-coloured background, while the back is striped in the same colours as the roses.

GETTING STARTED

Easy basic fabric for cushion cover but making roses may take some practice.

Size:
To fit a 30 x 60cm (12 x 24in) cushion pad

How much yarn:
3 x 50g (1¾oz) balls of Rowan Cashsoft DK in colour A – Cream (shade 500)
1 ball in each of six other colours: B – Spruce (shade 541); C – Poppy (shade 512); D – Kingfisher (shade 525); E – Lime (shade 509); F – Blue Jacket (shade 535); G – Opulence (shade 521)

Hook:
4.00mm (UK 8) crochet hook

Additional item:
30 x 60cm (12 x 24in) cushion pad

Tension:
18 sts and 14 rows measure 10cm (4in) square over htr on 4.00mm (UK 8) hook
IT IS ESSENTIAL TO WORK TO THE STATED TENSION TO ACHIEVE SUCCESS

What you have to do:
Work cushion back in half trebles and stripes of all colours except main colour. Work cushion front in half trebles and main colour only. Make thirteen roses in rounds as instructed and a variety of colours. Crochet back and front of cushion together with double crochet. Arrange roses on cushion front and sew in place.

The Yarn

Rowan Cashsoft DK (approx. 115m/125 yards per 50g/1¾oz ball) is a blend of 57% extra fine merino wool, 33% acrylic microfibre and 10% cashmere. It produces a soft, luxurious fabric that can be machine washed. There is a good range of neutral and more bold shades.

Instructions

Abbreviations:

ch = chain
cm = centimetre(s)
cont = continue
dc = double crochet
htr = half treble
patt = pattern
ss = slip stitch
st(s) = stitch(es)
tr = treble
WS = wrong side

BACK:

Note: When joining in a new colour, always work last part of last st in old colour with new colour.

With 4.00mm (UK 8) hook and B, make 101ch.

Foundation row: (WS) 1htr into 3rd ch from hook, 1htr into each ch to end, turn. 100 sts.

Patt row: 2ch (counts as first htr), miss st at base of ch, 1htr into each st to end, working last htr into 2nd of 2ch, turn.

Patt 1 more row.

Joining in and cutting off colours as required, cont in stripe sequence of 3 rows each C, D, E, F, G and B until third stripe in C has been completed. Fasten off.

FRONT:

With 4.00mm (UK 8) hook and A, make 101ch. Work foundation row and patt row as given for Back. Patt a further 40 rows. Fasten off.

ROSE: (make 13)

With 4.00mm (UK 8) hook and C, make 5ch, join with a ss into first ch to form a ring.

1st round: 1ch (counts as first dc), work 11dc into ring, join with a ss into first ch.

2nd round: 5ch, miss next dc, 1dc into next dc, (4ch, miss next dc, 1dc into next dc) 4 times, 4ch, join with a ss into first of 5ch.

3rd round: Work (1dc, 5tr and 1dc all into next ch loop) 6 times, join with a ss into first dc.
6 petals formed.

4th round: Working behind petals, 1dc into first of 5ch on 2nd round, (5ch, 1dc into next dc on 2nd round) 5 times, 5ch, join with a ss into first dc.

5th round: Work (1dc, 7tr and 1dc all into next ch loop) 6 times, join with a ss into first dc.

6th round: Working behind petals, 1dc into first dc on 4th round, (6ch, 1dc into next dc on 4th round) 5 times, 6ch, join with a ss into first dc.

7th round: Work (1dc, 9tr and 1dc all into next ch loop) 6 times, join with a ss into first dc. Fasten off. Make 2 more roses in C, then make 2 roses in each of B, D, E, F and G. 13 roses in total.

 Making up

Do not press. With 4.00mm (UK 8) hook, WS facing and working into both pieces, join A to one corner and work a round of dc evenly around outer edge to join back and front, leaving a gap to insert cushion pad. Insert pad and cont to join last edge, join with a ss into first dc. Fasten off. Pin roses to cushion front in arrangement as required and then sew in place.

Flower-trimmed mesh gloves

Step back in time with these pretty gloves.

These delicate mesh gloves in traditional ecru cotton have a frill at the wrist and are trimmed with pretty beaded flower motifs.

The Yarn

DMC Petra No. 5 (approx. 400m/436 yards per 100g/3½oz ball) is a fine, traditional mercerized 100% cotton. It produces a soft and supple fabric with a slight sheen that is ideal for elegant crochet projects. DMC Coton Perlé No.5 is a highly mercerized, twisted cotton thread that is suitable for embroidery or fine crochet work.

Instructions

LEFT GLOVE:
With 2.50mm (UK 12) hook make 50ch and beg at wrist.
Foundation row: (RS) 1tr in 6th ch from hook, *1ch, miss 1ch, 1tr in next ch, rep from * to end. 23 mesh sps. Now join work into a round as foll, forming the top of button opening:
1st round: Do not turn the work, 4ch (counts as 1tr and 1ch), form Foundation row into a circle without twisting so

RS of Foundation row is facing, work 1tr in 4th of 5ch at beg Foundation row, 1ch, miss 1ch, * 1tr in tr, 1ch, miss 1ch, rep from *, ending with 1ss in 3rd of 4ch at beg of round. 24 mesh sps.
Foll rounds beg and end at edge of palm, opposite thumb:**
Shape thumb gusset:
1st thumb round: 4ch, miss 1ch, (1tr in tr, 1ch, miss 1ch)

Abbreviations:

beg = beginning
ch = chain(s)
cm = centimetre(s)
dc = double crochet
dc2(3)tog = work 1dc into each of next 2(3) sts leaving last loop of each on hook, yrh and draw through all 3(4) loops
dtr = double treble
foll = follow(s)(ing)
htr = half treble
patt = pattern
rep = repeat
RS = right side
sp(s) = space(s)
ss = slip stitch
st(s) = stitch(es)
tog = together
tr = treble(s)
tr2(3)tog = work 1tr into each of next 2(3) sts leaving last loop of each on hook, yrh and draw through all 3(4) loops
WS = wrong side
yrh = yarn round hook

10 times, (1tr, 1ch) twice in next tr, (1tr in tr, 1ch, miss 1ch) 12 times, join with a ss in 3rd of 4ch.

2nd thumb round: 4ch, miss 1ch, (1tr in tr, 1ch, miss 1ch) 10 times, (1tr, 1ch) twice in each of next 2tr, (1tr in tr, 1ch, miss 1ch) 12 times, join with a ss in 3rd of 4ch.

3rd thumb round: 4ch, miss 1ch, (1tr in tr, 1ch, miss 1ch) 10 times, (1tr, 1ch) twice in next tr, (1tr in tr, 1ch, miss 1ch) twice, (1tr, 1ch) twice in next tr, (1tr in tr, 1ch, miss 1ch) 12 times, join with a ss in 3rd of 4ch.

4th thumb round: 4ch, miss 1ch, (1tr in tr, 1ch, miss 1ch) 10 times, (1tr, 1ch) twice in next tr, (1tr in tr, 1ch, miss 1ch) 4 times, (1tr, 1ch) twice in next tr, (1tr in tr, 1ch, miss 1ch) 12 times, join with a ss in 3rd of 4ch.

5th thumb round: 4ch, miss 1ch, (1tr in tr, 1ch, miss 1ch) 10 times, (1tr, 1ch) twice in next tr, (1tr in tr, 1ch, miss 1ch) 6 times, (1tr, 1ch) twice in next tr, (1tr in tr, 1ch, miss 1ch) 12 times, join with a ss in 3rd of 4ch. 33 mesh patts.

Mesh patt round: 4ch, miss 1ch, * 1tr in tr, 1ch, miss 1ch , rep from *, ending with 1ss in 3rd of 4ch at beg of round. Rep last round 3 more times.

Shape thumb hole:

Next round: 4ch, miss 1ch, (1tr in tr, 1ch, miss 1ch) 10 times, (1tr inserting hook in next tr and in foll 9th tr, leaving 8tr unworked), 1ch, 1tr in same place as last insertion, 1ch, (1tr in tr, 1ch, miss 1ch) 12 times, join with a ss in 3rd of 4ch. 25 mesh patts. Work mesh patt round 3 times.

Little finger:

1st round: 4ch, miss 1ch, (1tr in tr, 1ch, miss 1tr) 3 times, miss 18tr, (1tr in tr, 1ch, miss 1ch) 3 times, join with a ss in 3rd of 4ch. 7 mesh patts. Work mesh patt round 5 times.

Last round: 2ch, working in tr of previous round: (tr2tog) 3 times. Fasten off.

Ring finger:

1st round: With palm of glove facing, rejoin yarn to same tr as 3rd tr of 1st round of little finger, 4ch, miss 1ch, (1tr in tr, 1ch, miss 1ch) 3 times, miss 12tr, (1tr in tr, 1ch, miss 1ch) 3 times, 1tr in same tr as 4th tr of 1st round of little finger, 1ch, join with a ss in 3rd of 4ch. 8 mesh patts. Work mesh patt round 7 times.

Last round: 2ch, (tr2tog) twice, tr3tog. Fasten off.

Middle finger:

1st round: With palm of glove facing, rejoin yarn to same tr as 3rd tr of 1st round of ring finger, 4ch, miss 1ch, (1tr in tr, 1ch, miss 1ch) 3 times, miss 6tr, (1tr in tr, 1ch, miss 1ch) 3 times, 1tr in same tr as 4th tr of 1st round of ring finger, 1ch, join with a ss in 3rd of 4ch. 8 mesh patts. Work mesh patt round 8 times.

Last round: As given for ring finger.

Forefinger:

1st round: With palm of glove facing, rejoin yarn to same tr as 3rd tr of 1st round of middle finger, 4ch, miss 1ch, (1tr in tr, 1ch, miss 1ch) 6 times, 1tr in same tr as 4th tr of 1st round of middle finger, 1ch, join with a ss in 3rd of 4ch. 8 mesh patts. Work mesh patt round 7 times.

Last round: As given for ring finger.

Thumb:

1st round: With palm of glove facing, rejoin yarn to same tr as joined tr at inner edge of thumb hole, 4ch, miss 1ch, (1tr in tr, 1ch, miss 1ch) 8 times, join with a ss in 3rd of 4ch. 9 mesh patts. Work mesh patt round 5 times.

Last round: 2ch, tr2tog, (tr3tog) twice. Fasten off.

Wrist border:

With RS of glove facing, work along lower edge:

1st row: Join yarn to base of last tr of foundation row, 1ch (counts as first dc), 1dc in each ch sp and base of each tr all around, turn. 47 sts.

2nd row: 1ch, miss first dc, 1dc in each dc, ending with 1dc in 1ch, turn.

3rd and 4th rows: As 2nd row.

5th row: 2ch, 1tr in first dc, 3ch, *tr2tog over next 2dc, 3ch, rep from *, ending tr2tog over last dc and 1ch, turn.

6th row: 2ch, 1tr in first 3ch sp, *4ch, tr2tog over (same and next 3ch sp), rep from *, ending in last 3ch sp, 4ch, tr2tog over (same 3ch sp and tr at beg of 5th row), turn.

7th row: 2ch, 1tr in first 4ch sp, *5ch, tr2tog over (same and next 4ch sp), rep from *, ending in last 4ch sp, 5ch, tr2tog over (same 4ch sp and tr at beg of 6th row), turn.

8th row: 1ch, 1dc in first 5ch sp, *1ch, (1tr, 3dtr, 1tr) in same ch sp as last st, 1ch, dc2tog over (same and next 5ch sp), rep from *, ending 1ch, 1dc in last ch sp, 1dc in tr at beg of 7th row. Fasten off.

Border to button opening:

With RS of work facing, rejoin yarn at opposite end of wrist border.

1st row: 1ch (counts as first dc), work around edge of button opening as foll: 5dc in side edge of 3 frill rows, 4dc in side edge of dc rows, 4dc in side edge of 2 mesh rows, 1dc at top of opening, 4dc in side edge of 2 mesh rows, 2dc in side edge of first 2dc rows, 4ch, 2dc in side edge of 2 dc rows, 6dc in side edge of 3 frill rows, turn.

2nd row: 1ch, miss first dc, 1dc in each of 7dc to ch loop, dc2tog over (same place as last dc, and into ch loop), 2dc in ch loop, dc2tog over (ch loop and next dc), 1dc in same place, 1dc in each of 4dc, dc3tog over next 3dc, 1dc in each dc, ending 1dc in 1ch.
Fasten off.

RIGHT GLOVE:

Work as for Left glove to **.

Shape thumb gusset:

Complete to match Left glove, reversing shaping by working 13 mesh patts before shaping thumb gusset (and 11 mesh patts after). Start the rounds for fingers with back of glove facing (instead of palm).

Work wrist border as given. Work button opening to match Left glove, but with ch loop on opposite side of opening.

FLOWERS: (make 2 in each contrast colour)

Make a magic circle (see Note on page 54).

1st round: With 2.50mm (UK 12) hook, work 5ch (counts as 1htr, 3ch), (1htr, 3ch) 4 times, pull gently on yarn tail to close centre, join with a ss in 2nd of 5ch. 5 ch sps.

2nd round: Ss in first 3ch sp, *1ch, (1tr, 1dtr, 1tr) in same ch sp, 1ch, dc2tog over (same and next 3ch sp), rep from * 4 more times, ending last rep with 1dc in last ch sp, join with a ss in first ch. Fasten off.

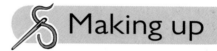

Making up

Thread tails at tops of fingers and thumb through tops of last round of sts, pull up and secure on WS. Use starting tails for fingers and thumb to close gaps between fingers.
Sew on buttons to match buttonholes.
Sew three flowers (one in each colour) to back of dc band of wrist border on each glove, with a bead at centre of each flower if desired.

Flower-sprinkled bag

Six-petalled flowers in toning pink shades decorate this bag.

This simple cotton bag in a mesh pattern is lined with fabric. It has an abundance of flowers in two toning shades worked directly on to the squares of the mesh.

GETTING STARTED

★ ★ *Bag is simple mesh pattern but care is needed with working flowers.*

Size:
23cm (9in) wide x 30cm (12in) deep, excluding handle

How much yarn:
2 x 50g (1¾oz) balls of DMC Natura Just Cotton in colour A – Eucaliptus (shade 8)
1 ball in each of colour B – Rose Soraya (shade 32) and colour C – Amaranto (shade 33)

Hook:
3.00mm (UK 11) crochet hook

Additional items:
60cm (¾ yard) of thick piping cord
26 x 62cm (10½ x 24½in) rectangle of lining fabric to match colour A
Matching sewing thread and needle

Tension:
24 sts (12 squares) and 11 rows measure 10cm (4in) over mesh pattern on 3.00mm (UK 11) hook
IT IS ESSENTIAL TO WORK TO THE STATED TENSION TO ACHIEVE SUCCESS

What you have to do:
Make back and front in mesh pattern with open squares. Work flowers directly on to mesh pattern of bag front as directed. Crochet back and front of bag together. Cover piping cord with strip of crochet trebles fabric. Sew simple fabric lining for bag.

The Yarn
DMC Natura Just Cotton (approx. 155m/169 yards per 50g/1¾oz ball) is 100% cotton with a matt finish. Although soft, it is strong. There are 34 vibrant shades to choose from.

Instructions

Abbreviations:

beg = beginning
ch = chain(s)
cm = centimetre(s)
cont = continue
dc = double crochet
dtr cl = double treble
cluster: *yrh twice, insert
hook as indicated, yrh
and pull through, (yrh
and pull through 2 loops)
twice, rep from * once
more, yrh and pull through
all 3 loops on hook
rep = repeat
RS = right side
ss = slip stitch
st(s) = stitch(es)
tog = together
tr = treble
WS = wrong side
yrh = yarn round hook

BACK:

With 3.00mm (UK 11) hook and A, make 57ch.

Foundation row: (RS) 1tr into 4th ch from hook, 1tr into each ch to end, turn.

1st row: 2ch (counts as first tr), miss st at base of ch, 1tr into each of next 2tr, (1ch, miss next tr, 1tr into next tr) 25 times, 1tr into next tr, 1tr into 3rd of 3ch, turn. 25 open squares.

2nd row: 2ch, miss st at base of ch, 1tr into each of next 2tr, (1ch, 1tr into next tr) 25 times, 1tr into next tr, 1tr into 2nd of 2ch, turn.

Rep last row 29 times more. 31 open

squares in depth.

32nd row: 2ch, miss st at base of ch, 1tr into each st to end. 55 sts. Fasten off.

FRONT:

Work as given for Back.

Flowers: (make 32)

Note: Flowers are worked around an open square each time.

With 3.00mm (UK 11) hook and RS of work facing, count 4 squares in from top and from right border and insert hook in this square. Using diagram 2 as a guide and holding B on RS of work, take hook underneath tr that forms right-hand side

Diagram I

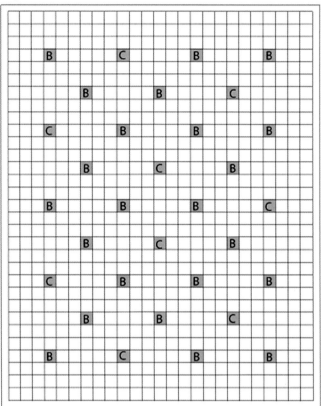

Diagram 2

 Making up

Place back and front together with WS facing. With 3.00mm (UK 11) hook, A and RS of front facing, join back to front by working 2dc around each pair of end sts to corner, work 4dc into last pair of sts, 1dc into each of base ch, 4dc into first pair of sts on second side, 2dc into each pair of end sts to top edge, do not fasten off. Starting 1ch, work 1dc into each st around top (including one st in each seam), join with a ss into first ch. Fasten off, leaving a long end.

To attach handle, insert each end of handle to depth of border and use long ends to sew them securely at end of handle and again at top of border, working in back stitch under ch of border.

Lining:

Fold lining fabric in half widthways and sew side seams to fit bag. Trim side turnings and over-sew edges. Slip lining into bag, turn under top edge and catch down along base of top tr border and around ends of handles.

of square and pull yarn through; around the tr work (3ch, dtr cl, 3ch, ss) twice; in 1ch that forms top of square (ss, 3ch, dtr cl, 3ch, ss); in tr that forms left-hand side of square (ss, 3ch, dtr cl, 3ch, ss) twice; in 1ch that forms base of square (ss, 3ch, dtr cl, 3ch, ss); fasten off by pulling yarn through loop on hook and leaving a long end for sewing. Attach tips of petals by threading end on to wool needle and making a single stitch into part of mesh indicated in diagram 2 and into top of dtr cl. Cont to make 32 flowers in this way with B and C, using diagram 1 as a guide to positioning.

HANDLE:

With 3.00mm (UK 11) hook and A, make 9ch.

Foundation row: 1tr into 4th ch from hook, 1tr into each ch to end, turn. 7 sts.

1st row: 2ch (counts as first tr), miss st at base of ch, 1tr into each st to end, working last tr into turning ch, turn. Rep last row until work measures 48cm (19cm) from beg. Do not fasten off. Fold strip lengthways around piping cord and, working 2dc around each pair of row-ends, join long edges with dc. Fasten off, leaving a long end. Trim ends of piping cord to same length as crochet.

Garden kneeler

Weeding will not feel so much of a chore with this daisy-themed kneeler.

This attractive kneeling pad for the garden is worked in double crochet and has blocks of bright, summery colours decorated with daisy motifs.

GETTING STARTED

★ ★ *Easy double crochet fabric with little shaping but intarsia colour work will require practice.*

Size:
Finished size is approximately 40cm (16in) long x 30cm (12in) wide (excluding handles)

How much yarn:
3 x 50g (1¾oz) balls of Rowan Handknit Cotton in each of colour A – Turkish Plum (shade 277) and colour B – Mist (shade 341)
1 ball in each of four other colours: C – Sea Foam (shade 352); D – Gooseberry (shade 219); E – Ochre (shade 349) and F – Bleached (shade 263)

Hook:
3.50mm (UK 9) crochet hook

Additional items:
Blunt tapestry needle
3 round buttons, 25mm (1in) in diameter
Cushion pad, 40 x 30cm (16 x 12in)
Plastic bubble wrap (optional)

Tension:
18 sts and 24 rows measure 10cm (4in) square over dc on 3.50mm (UK 9) hook
IT IS ESSENTIAL TO WORK TO THE STATED TENSION TO ACHIEVE SUCCESS

What you have to do:
Work throughout in double crochet with intarsia colour blocks on front of kneeler. Make separate daisy motifs and sew on to each colour block. Work handles and button covers in rounds.

The Yarn
Rowan Handknit Cotton (approx. 85m/93 yards per 50g/1¾oz ball) contains 100% cotton. It produces a hardwearing, versatile, machine-washable fabric with a matt finish. There is a wide range of colours.

 Instructions

Note: Use a separate ball of yarn for each area of colour. When changing colour, always twist yarns tog on WS of work to avoid holes forming.

COVER: (worked in one piece)
With 3.50mm (UK 9) hook and A, make 52ch.
1st row: (RS) 1dc into 2nd ch from hook, 1dc into each ch to end, turn.
2nd row: 1ch (does not count as a st), 1dc into each dc to end, turn. 51 sts.

Abbreviations:
ch = chain(s)
cm = centimetre(s)
dc = double crochet
foll = follows
rep = repeat
RS = right side
ss = slip stitch
st(s) = stitch(es)
tog = together
WS = wrong side

Rep last row 14 times more, cutting off yarn A and changing to B on last part of last st in A.

17–20th rows: With B, work 4 rows in dc.

21st row: 1ch, 1dc into each of first 3 sts joining in C on last st, with C, 1dc into each of next 21 sts, joining in another ball of B on last st, with B, 1dc into each of next 3 sts, joining in D on last st, with D, 1dc into each of next 21 sts, joining in another ball of B on last st, with B, 1dc into each of last 3 sts, turn.

22nd–46th rows: Work 25 rows in dc

in colours as set. Cut off C and D.

47th–50th rows: With B, work 4 rows in dc.

51st row: With B, 1ch, 1dc into each of first 3 sts, join in D on last st, with D, 1dc into each of next 21 sts, carry separate ball of B from previous colour change row up back of work and join in on last st, with B, 1dc into each of next 3 sts, join in C on last st, with C, 1dc into each of next 21 sts, carry separate ball of B from previous colour change row up back of work and join in on last st, with B, 1dc into each of last 3 sts, turn.

52nd–76th rows: Work 25 rows in colours as set. Cut off C and D.

77th–80th rows: With B, work 4 rows in dc, changing to A on last part of last st.

81st–96th rows: With A, work 16 rows in dc.

Back flap:

97th row: 1ch, 1dc into back loop only of each st to end, turn.

98th–112th rows: With B, work 15 rows in dc.

113th row: (buttonholes) 1ch, 1dc into each of first 7 sts, (5ch, miss next 5 sts,

1dc into each of next 11 sts) twice, 5ch, miss next 5 sts, 1dc into each of last 7 sts, turn.

114th row: 1ch, 1dc into each st and 5dc into each 5ch loop to end. Fasten off.

Back:

With RS facing, join A to foundation ch and working along opposite edge of ch, work 1ch (does not count as a st), 1dc into each ch to end, turn. 51 sts.

Work 15 rows in dc, changing to B on last part of last st. Work 60 rows in B.

Next row: 1ch, 1dc into each of next 49 sts, turn.

Next row: 1ch, 1dc into each of next 47 sts, turn.

Work 6 more rows in dc on these 47 sts. Fasten off.

HANDLES: (make 2)

With 3.50mm (UK 9) hook and A, make 54ch, join with a ss into first ch to form a ring.

1st round: 1ch (does not count as a st), 2dc into first ch, 1dc into each of next 8ch, (2dc into next ch, 1dc into each of next 8ch) 5 times, join with a ss into first dc. 60dc.

2nd round: 1ch, 2dc into first dc, 1dc into each of next 9dc, (2dc into next dc, 1dc into each of next 9dc) 5 times, join with a ss into first dc. 66dc.

3rd round: 1ch, 2dc into first dc, 1dc into each of next 10dc, (2dc into next dc, 1dc into each of next 10dc) 5 times, join with a ss into first dc. 72dc.

4th round: 1ch, 2dc in first dc, 1dc into each of next 11dc, (2dc into next dc, 1dc into each of next 11dc) 5 times, join with a ss into first dc. 78dc. Fasten off.

DAISIES: (make 4)

With 3.50mm (UK 9) hook and E, make a magic circle (see Note on page 54) and work 1ch (does not count as a st), 6dc into loop, join with a ss into first dc; pull tail of yarn to close up hole.

1st round: 1ch, 2dc into each dc, join with a ss into first dc. 12 sts. *

2nd round: 1ch, 2dc into first st, 1dc into next st, (2dc into next st, 1dc in next st) 5 times, join with a ss into first dc. 18 sts. Fasten off.

3rd round: (petals) Join in F and work (7ch, 1dc into 2nd ch from hook, 1dc into each of next 5ch, ss into next dc) 18 times. Fasten off.

BUTTON COVERs: (make 3)

Work as given for Daisy to *.

Next round: 1ch, 1dc into each dc, join with a ss into first dc. Fasten off, leaving a long tail.

Making up

Sew one daisy to centre of each coloured square, leaving tip of petals free.

With RS facing, fold down flap along ridge formed by row worked into back loops only, then fold up Back at foundation ch. Leaving last 8 rows of Back free, oversew side edges and edges of back flap using matching yarns. Fold each handle in half, matching corners, and oversew stitches together on outer and inner edges. Stitch folded ends of handles to folded edges of cover.

For buttons, thread tail of yarn into a blunt tapestry needle and thread through loops around perimeter of circle, then place button in centre and pull up yarn to gather around button. Sew on buttons to correspond with buttonholes.

Before inserting cushion pad, wrap it in plastic bubble wrap to protect it from damp when used on wet ground.

Beads and flowers hair clip

Pin up your hair with this unusual ornament.

Worked in subtle shaded colours of embroidery thread and sprinkled with beads, this hair decoration is perfect for evening wear.

GETTING STARTED

★★ *Very fine work with embroidery thread but motifs are not difficult to make; careful assembly is required.*

Size:
Approximately 12cm (4¾in) x 6cm (2½in)

How much yarn:
1 skein of DMC Color Variations thread in each of six colours: A – Coral (shade 4190); B – Cream (shade 4160); C – Lemon (shade 4077); D – Blue (shade 4030); E – Dark Green (shade 4045) and F – Light Green (shade 4065)

Hook:
2.00mm (UK 14) crochet hook

Additional items:
Hair slide, fabric covered and measuring approximately 8 x 2cm (3 x ¾in)
8 pink and 6 green 2mm (⅛in) rocaille beads
8mm (⁵⁄₁₆in) flat-backed pink diamante bead
2 x 4mm (¼in) flat-backed pink diamante beads
Sewing needle and matching thread

What you have to do:
Make large and small flowers in rounds as directed and sew beads at their centres. Make a selection of fern 'fronds'. Assemble and sew arrangement of motifs onto hair clip. Decorate by sewing on more small beads.

The Yarn
DMC Color Variations is a 100% cotton embroidery thread. There are 36 shades in the range, each consisting of a succession of subtle shaded colours that change every few stitches.

Instructions

Abbreviations:
ch = chain(s)
cm = centimetre(s)
dc = double crochet
dtr = double treble
rep = repeat
sps = spaces
ss = slip stitch
tr = treble
tr-tr = triple treble

LARGE FLOWER:
Main flower:
With 2.00mm (UK 14) hook and A, make 6ch, join with a ss in first ch to form a ring.
1st round: 6ch, (1tr in ring, 3ch) 7 times, join with a ss into 3rd of 6ch. 8 ch sps.
2nd round: In each 3ch sp work (2ch, 1tr, 1dtr, 1tr-tr, 1dtr, 1tr, 1dc).
Fasten off.
3rd round: Join B to any dc, (1dc in dc, 1dc in 2nd ch, 1dc in tr, 1dc in dtr, (1dc, 1ch, 1dc) in tr-tr, 1dc in dtr, 1dc in tr) 8 times.
Fasten off.
Flower centre:
With 2.00mm (UK 14) hook and C, make 6ch, join with a ss in first ch to form a ring.
1st round: In ring work 1dc, (1tr, 1dtr, 1ch, 1dtr, 1tr, 1dc) 6 times.
Fasten off.
Sew flower centre to main flower, then sew 8mm (⁵⁄₁₆in) diamante bead securely in centre through both layers.

SMALL FLOWER: (make 2)
Work Main flower as given for Large flower, making 6 petals instead of 8.
Flower centre:
With 2.00mm (UK 14) hook and C, make 4ch, join with a ss in first ch to form a ring.
1st round: (3ch, ss in ring) 9 times.
Fasten off.
Sew flower centre to main flower, then sew 4mm (¼in) diamante bead securely in centre through both layers.

BLUE FLOWERS: (make 4)
With 2.00mm (UK 14) hook and D, make 5ch, join with a ss in first ch to form a ring.
1st round: (5ch, ss in ring) 9 times.
Fasten off.

3-FROND FERN: (make 3 in E and 1 in F)
With 2.00mm (UK 14) hook, *make 10ch, ss in 4th ch from hook, (6ch, ss in 4th ch

from hook) twice, (4ch, ss in 4th ch from hook) twice, ss in each of next 2ch, (4ch, ss in 4th ch from hook, ss in each of next 2ch) twice, ss in each of next 4ch **, rep from * twice more to make two more fronds. Fasten off.

SINGLE-FROND FERN:
(make 1 in E and 1 in F)
Work as given for 3-frond fern to **.
Fasten off.

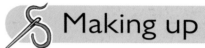 ## Making up

Using photograph as a guide, sew large flower to centre of clip, then sew two blue flowers to left and other two to right. Sew small flowers on either side. Add fern fronds, sewing them to back of petals. Position one 3-frond fern at top of each small flower and other two below them. Sew two single fronds to lower edge of large flower. Sew a sprinkling of pink beads around centre flower and small flowers and green beads around blue flowers.

Heart-shaped purse

Get stitching to make the perfect little present.

This cute purse that hangs from a wrist strap is worked in cotton yarn and has extra embellishments on the front. Lined with matching fabric, it has a zipped side opening.

The Yarn

Rico Essentials Cotton DK (approx. 130m/142 yards per 50g/1¾oz ball) contains 100% mercerized cotton. It produces a smooth fabric with a delicate sheen, ideal for craft projects. There is a wide shade palette.

GETTING STARTED

 Small item but needs careful construction and basic sewing skills for a good result.

Size:
Heart measures approximately 11.5cm (4½in) in diameter x 11cm (4¼in) in depth

How much yarn:
1 x 50g (1¾oz) ball of Rico Essentials Cotton DK in each of three colours: A – Fuchsia (shade 14), B – Cherry (shade 04) and C – Rose (shade 01)

Hooks:
4.00mm (UK 8) crochet hook
4.50mm (UK 7) crochet hook

Additional items:
2 x 15cm (6in) squares of pink cotton lining fabric
1 x 4cm (1½in) square of pink cotton lining fabric for zip tab

1 x 15cm (6in) pink zip fastener
Pink sewing thread and needle
Scrap paper for template and pencil
Fabric marker

Tension:
Heart measures 5cm (2in) wide and 4cm (1½in) tall after 1st round on 4.00mm (UK 8) hook
IT IS ESSENTIAL TO WORK TO THE STATED TENSION TO ACHIEVE SUCCESS

What you have to do:
Work front and back of purse in rounds of trebles, shaping as indicated. Using contrast colours, make heart motif and bobbles for purse front and sew in place. Sew fabric lining with zip fastener for purse.

Instructions

Abbreviations:
beg = beginning
ch = chain(s)
cm = centimetre(s)
cont = continue
dc = double crochet
foll = follow(s)(ing)
rep = repeat
RS = right side
ss = slip stitch
st(s) = stitch(es)
tr = treble
tr5tog = (yrh, insert hook as indicated, yrh and draw through a loop, yrh and draw through first two loops on hook) 5 times, yrh and draw through all 6 loops on hook
WS = wrong side
yrh = yarn round hook

PURSE: (make 2)
With 4.50mm (UK 7) hook and A, make 12ch. Change to 4.00mm (UK 8) hook.

1st round: 2tr into 4th ch from hook, 2tr into next ch, tr5tog over next 5ch, 2tr into next ch, 5tr into last ch, then work back along underside of foundation ch as foll: 2tr into next ch, 1tr into each of next 2ch, 5tr into foll ch, 1tr into each of next 2ch, 2tr into each of last 2ch,

join with a ss into 3rd of 3ch at start of round. 28 sts.

2nd round: 3ch (counts as first tr), 1tr into st at base of ch, 2tr into each of next 2 sts, tr5tog over next 5 sts, 2tr into each of foll 5 sts, 1tr into each of next 6 sts, 5tr into foll st, 1tr into each of next 6 sts, 2tr into each of foll 2 sts, join with a ss into 3rd of 3ch. 38 sts.

3rd round: 3ch, 1tr into st at base of ch, 2tr into each of next 3 sts, tr5tog over next 5 sts, 2tr into each of foll 7 sts, 1tr into each of next 9 sts, 5tr into foll st, 1tr into each of next 9 sts, 2tr into each of foll 3 sts, join with a ss into 3rd of 3ch. 52 sts.

4th round: 3ch, 1tr into st at base of ch, 2tr into each of next 4 sts, 1tr into foll st, tr5tog over next 5 sts, 1tr into foll st, 2tr into each of next 9 sts, 1tr into each of foll 13 sts, 5tr into next st, 1tr into each of foll 13 sts, 2tr into each of next 4 sts, join with a ss into 3rd of 3ch. 70 sts. Fasten off.

Heart motif:
With 4.00mm (UK 8) hook and B, make 12ch. Work 1st round as given for Purse. Fasten off, leaving a long end. Align with centre of heart on Purse front and sew in place.

Bobbles: (make 10)
With 4.00mm hook and C, make a magic circle (see Note on page 54). Work 7dc into ring, join with a ss into first dc, then tighten yarn end to close ring. Fasten off, leaving a long end. Using picture as a guide, position bobbles on 3rd round of Purse front, spacing them evenly, and use yarn end to sew in place.

WRIST LOOP:

With 4.00mm (UK 8) hook and A, make 4ch, yrh, insert hook into 4th ch from hook and pull loop through, *yrh and draw through first loop on hook (to form a ch into which next rep is worked), (yrh and draw through first 2 loops on hook) twice, yrh, insert hook into ch indicated and pull loop through, rep from * until loop measures 25cm (10in) from beg. Fasten off.

Sew ends together to form a loop.

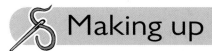 ## Making up

Lining:

Make a heart template by drawing around one Purse heart on scrap paper and cut out. Place pink lining squares together with RS facing and raw edges matching. Place heart template centrally on top and cut out, adding 1cm (⅜in) extra all around for seam allowance. Place template on RS of each heart lining and draw around it with fabric marker. Make small notches in seam allowance around curved edge.

Fold 4cm (1½in) square of lining fabric for zip tab in half. Place folded edge across top of closed zip, directly above zip pull, and sew securely across. Trim off excess leaving 1cm (⅜in) allowance.

Position zip, RS up, around right edge of heart lining (RS facing), with zip end as near lower corner point as possible and zip following marked line around, tacking in place as you work; sew in place. With RS facing, position other heart lining on top and sew zip in place as before. Sew around rest of heart lining, from lower corner point of zip around to top, ending just before zip tab and working 1cm (⅜in) in from outer edge.

Purse:

With WS of crochet hearts facing and using A, whip stitch together, beg at lower corner point and finishing at top dip but do not fasten off. Insert wrist loop into space at top dip and sew securely in place. Slip fabric lining into purse to check where zip ends and if necessary cont sewing round to zip side. Fasten off securely.

With fabric lining in place, align zip to open edges of purse and pin in place, tucking zip edges and fabric zip tab neatly inside. Undo zip and slip stich zip tape neatly in place 5mm (¼in) from zip teeth, taking care not to catch fabric lining inside.

Spring fever scarf

Framed flowers are the theme for this delicate
fair-weather scarf.

This long and narrow tassel-trimmed scarf, worked in a soft cotton yarn, features colourful square motifs with a raised flower design at the centre set within a border of trebles.

The Yarn

King Cole Bamboo Cotton DK (approx. 230m/251 yards per 100g/3½oz ball) contains 50% bamboo and 50% cotton. It produces a soft machine-washable fabric and there is a wide range of colours to choose from.

GETTING STARTED

 Although squares are relatively easy, concentration is required to construct flower at centre.

Size:

9.5cm (3¾in) wide x 110cm (43in) long, excluding tassels

How much yarn:

1 x 100g (3½oz) ball of King Cole Bamboo Cotton DK in each of four colours: A – Oyster (shade 543); B – Violet (shade 537); C – Moss (shade 526) and D – Opal (shade 527)

Hook:

3.50mm (UK 9) crochet hook

Tension:

One square measures 7.5cm (3in) on 3.50mm (UK 9) hook
IT IS ESSENTIAL TO WORK TO THE STATED TENSION TO ACHIEVE SUCCESS

What you have to do:

Use four colours to make six squares with raised flower motif in centre. Use same colours to make another six squares but alternating the colours. Join squares by working treble edging along one side of square and sewing to next square. Work a border in trebles around scarf. Make tassels and knot along both short ends.

Instructions

Abbreviations:

beg = beginning
ch = chain(s)
cm = centimetre(s)
dc = double crochet
foll = follows
htr = half treble
rep = repeat
RS = right side
sp(s) = space(s)
ss = slip stitch
st(s) = stitch(es)
tr = treble

FLORAL SQUARE 1: (make 6)
With 3.50mm (UK 9) hook and A, make 4ch, join with a ss into first ch to form a ring.
1st round: 3ch (counts as first tr), 3tr into ring, 1ss into ring, *4tr into ring, 1ss into ring, rep from * twice more. Fasten off A. 4 small petals.
2nd round: Join B with a ss to back of st in middle of first petal, *3ch, ss into back of st in middle of next petal, rep from * 3 more times, working last ss into ss at beg of round.
Four 3ch sps.
3rd round: Into each 3ch sp, work (1dc, 3htr, 1dc, 1ss). Fasten off.
4 larger petals.
4th round: Join C with a ss to back of first ss in previous round, *6ch, ss into back of ss between petals, rep from * 3 more times, working last ss into ss at beg of round. Four 6ch sps.

5th round: Ss into first 6ch sp, 3ch, (2tr, 3ch, 3tr) into same sp, *1ch, (3tr, 3ch, 3tr) into next 6ch sp, rep from * twice more, 1ch, join with a ss into 3rd of 3ch. Fasten off.

6th round: Join D with a ss to 3ch (corner) sp, 3ch, (2tr, 3ch, 3tr) into same sp, 1tr into each of next 3tr, 1tr into 1ch sp, 1tr into each of next 3tr, *(3tr, 3ch, 3tr) into next 3ch sp, 1tr into each of next 3tr, 1tr into 1ch sp, 1tr into each of next 3tr, rep from * twice more, join with a ss into 3rd of 3ch. Fasten off.

FLORAL SQUARE 2: (make 6)

With 3.50mm (UK 9) hook and B, make 4ch, join with a ss into first ch to form a ring. Work as given for Floral square 1, working rounds in colours as foll:
1st round: B; 2nd and 3rd rounds: A; 4th and 5th rounds: D and 6th round: C.

 ## Making up

Join squares as foll: With 3.50mm (UK 9) hook and RS of one Floral square 2 facing, join B with a ss to 3ch sp at top right corner of square, 3ch (counts as first tr), 1tr into each tr to next corner, 1tr into corner 3ch sp. 15 sts. Fasten off, leaving a long tail. Use tail to whip stitch square to lower edge of one Floral square 1. Alternating squares, rep this sequence of working tr edging along top of last joined square and sewing it to lower edge of next square until all squares have been joined.

Border:

With 3.50mm (UK 9) hook and RS of work facing, join B with a ss to 3ch sp at top right corner of one short end of scarf, 3ch, (2tr, 3ch, 3tr) into same sp, *1tr into each of next 13tr, (3tr, 3ch, 3tr) into next corner 3ch sp, (1tr into each of next 13tr, 2tr into 3ch sp, 2tr over bar of end tr of edging row, 2tr into next 3ch sp) to next corner 3ch sp *, (3tr, 3ch, 3tr) into corner sp, rep from * to * again, join with a ss into 3rd of 3ch. Fasten off.

Tassels: (make 8)

For each tassel, cut 6 x 30cm (12in) lengths of B. At one short end of scarf, knot one tassel into 3ch sp at each corner with two more evenly spaced between. Repeat to knot four tassels at other short end.

Flower band hat

Crochet this pretty pull-on hat in next-to-no time.

Patterned with crossed trebles, this hat has a floppy brim worked in plain double crochet. The integral hatband is decorated with a row of flower motifs, made separately and sewn on.

GETTING STARTED

★ ★ *Working in rounds may take some practice but the rest is straightforward.*

Size:
To fit head with approximate circumference of 56cm (22in)

How much yarn:
3 x 50g (1¾oz) balls of Debbie Bliss Eco Aran in colour A – Rice (shade 631)
1 ball in colour B – Raspberry (shade 625)

Hook:
4.00mm (UK 8) crochet hook

Tension:
Work measures 16cm (6¼in) in diameter after completion of 6th round on 4.00mm (UK 8) hook
IT IS ESSENTIAL TO WORK TO THE STATED TENSION TO ACHIEVE SUCCESS

What you have to do:
Work throughout in rounds. Start at crown and work in trebles, increasing as directed. Work crossed trebles pattern around sides with 'band' in a contrast colour. Work brim in double crochet, increasing as directed. Make separate flower motifs and sew on to hat band.

The Yarn
Debbie Bliss Eco Aran (approx. 75m/82 yards per 50g/1¾oz ball) contains 100% organic cotton. This soft cotton yarn produces a smooth, thick fabric that is comfortable to wear on the head and can be machine washed. There is a good range of exciting colours.

Instructions

Abbreviations:

beg = begin
ch = chain
cont = continue
dc = double crochet
foll = follows
htr = half treble
patt = pattern
rep = repeat
sp(s) = space(s)
ss = slip stitch
st(s) = stitch(es)
tr = treble

HAT:

With 4.00mm (UK 8) hook and A, make 4ch and beg at centre of crown.

1st round: Work 11tr into 4th ch from hook, join with a ss into 3rd of 3ch. 12 sts.

2nd round: 3ch (counts as first tr), 2tr into each st to end, 1tr into st at base of 3ch, join with a ss into 3rd of 3ch. 24 sts.

3rd round: 3ch, 2tr into next st, *1tr into next st, 2tr into next st, rep from * to end, join with a ss into 3rd of 3ch. 36 sts.

4th round: 3ch, 1tr into next st, 2tr into next st, *1tr into each of next 2 sts, 2tr into next st, rep from * to end, join with a ss into 3rd of 3ch. 48 sts.

5th round: 3ch, 1tr into each of next 2 sts, 2tr into next st, *1tr into each of next 3 sts, 2tr into next st, rep from * to end, join with a ss into 3rd of 3ch. 60 sts.

6th round: 3ch, 1tr into each of next 3 sts, 2tr into next st, *1tr into each of next 4 sts, 2tr into next st, rep from * to end, join with a ss into 3rd of 3ch. 72 sts.

Cont in crossed tr patt as foll:

7th–9th rounds: 3ch, 1tr into st before 3ch, *miss next st, 1tr into next st, 1tr into missed st, rep from * to end, join with a ss into 3rd of 3ch. 36 crossed tr.

10th and 11th rounds: 3ch, 1tr into each st to end, join with a ss into 3rd of 3ch. 72 sts.

12th–14th rounds: As 7th–9th rounds.

15th round: As 10th round, changing to B on last st.

16th round: With B, 1ch (does not count as a st), 1dc into first st, 1dc into each st to end, join with a ss into first dc.

17th round: With B, as 7th round, changing to A on last st. Cut off B and cont in A only.

Brim:

18th round: 1ch, *1dc into each of next 2 sts, 2dc into next st, rep from * to end, join with a ss into first dc. 96 sts.

19th round: 1ch, 1dc into each st to end, join with a ss into first dc.

20th round: As 18th round. 128 sts.

21st–24th rounds: As 19th round. Fasten off.

FLOWER MOTIF: (make 2 using A as 1st colour and B as 2nd colour and 1 using B as 1st colour and A as 2nd colour)

With 4.00mm (UK 8) hook and 1st colour, make 4ch, join with a ss into first ch to form a ring.

1st round: Work 8dc into ring, changing to 2nd colour, join with a ss into first dc.

2nd round: With 2nd colour, *3ch, miss next st, 1dc into next st, rep from * to end. Four 3ch sps.

3rd round: Into each 3ch sp work (1ss, 1dc, 1htr, 1tr, 1htr, 1dc, 1ss), join with a ss into first ss. Fasten off leaving a long end.

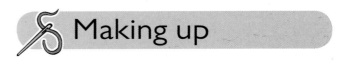

Making up

Using photograph as a guide, use long ends to sew flower motifs in a line on to band of hat.

Funky tea cosy

Brighten up your cup of tea and the afternoon with this amazing flower-decorated cosy.

Make a cup of tea a talking point with this grass green lacy-patterned cosy with its drawstring top sprouting brightly coloured crochet flowers.

GETTING STARTED

⭐ *Fabric and flowers are easy to work and cosy requires no shaping.*

Size:
Finished cosy is approximately 23cm (9in) tall and 42cm (16½in) in circumference

How much yarn:
2 x 50g (1¾oz) balls of Debbie Bliss Cashmerino Aran in main colour A – Green (shade 502)
1 x 50g (1¾oz) ball of Debbie Bliss Cashmerino DK in each of three contrast colours: B – Pale Blue (shade 09); C – Orange (shade 14) and D – Aubergine (shade 32)

Hook:
5.00mm (UK 6) crochet hook

Additional items:
46 x 25cm (18 x 10in) rectangle of cotton lining fabric Matching thread and sewing needle, one button

Tension:
12 sts (1 patt rep) and measures 7cm (2¾in) and 6 rows measure 10cm (4in) over patt on 5.00mm (UK 6) hook
IT IS ESSENTIAL TO WORK TO THE STATED TENSION TO ACHIEVE SUCCESS

What you have to do:
Make foundation chain. Work in pattern as instructed. Make lengths of chain and plait for drawstring. Make and sew on flowers in various colours for decoration. Sew simple fabric lining into tea cosy.

The Yarn
Debbie Bliss Cashmerino Aran (approx. 90m/98 yards per 50g/1¾oz ball) and DK (approx. 110m/120 yards per 50g/1¾oz ball) both contain 55% merino wool, 33% microfibre and 12% cashmere and are machine-washable.

Instructions

Abbreviations:

beg = beginning
ch = chain(s)
cm = centimetre(s)
dc = double crochet
patt = pattern
rep = repeat
RS = right side
sp = space
ss = slip stitch
st(s) = stitch(es)
tr = treble
WS = wrong side

TEA COSY: (make 2 pieces)

With 5.00mm (UK 6) hook and A, make 34ch.

Foundation row: (RS) Work 2tr into 4th ch from hook, *miss 4ch, (1tr, 3ch, 1tr) all into next ch, miss 4ch, (3tr, 1ch, 3tr) all into next ch, rep from * once, miss 4ch, (1tr, 3ch, 1tr) all into next ch, miss 4ch, 3tr into last ch, turn.

1st row: 4ch (counts as first tr and 1ch), 1tr into first tr, *(3tr, 1ch, 3tr) all into next ch sp, (1tr, 3ch, 1tr) all into next ch sp, rep from * ending with (1tr, 1ch, 1tr) into 3rd of 3ch, turn.

2nd row: 3ch (counts as first tr), 2tr into first ch sp, *(1tr, 3ch, 1tr) into next ch sp, (3tr, 1ch, 3tr) into next ch sp, rep from * ending with 3tr into 3rd of 4ch, turn. The 1st and 2nd rows form patt. Rep them until work measures approximately 23cm (9in) from beg, ending with a 1st row. Fasten off.

DRAWSTRING:

With 5.00mm (UK 6) hook and C, make 3 lengths of ch approximately 70cm (28in) in length. Take start of each ch length and sew together with a few sts leaving end 3cm (1¼in) free on 1st length, 4cm (1½in) free on 2nd length and 5cm (2in) free on 3rd. Plait lengths together and, staggering ends as before, secure with a few sts.

FLOWERS:

1st Flower: (make 2)

With 5.00mm (UK 6) hook and B, make 6ch, join with a ss into first ch to form a ring.

1st round: Work 1ch, 18dc into ring, join with a ss into first dc.

2nd round: 1ch, 1dc into first dc, *5ch, miss 2dc, 1dc into next dc, rep from * to end omitting 1dc at end of last rep, ss into first dc. Fasten off.

2nd Flower: (make 2)
With 5.00mm (UK 6) hook and C, make 6ch, join with a ss into first ch to form a ring.

1st round: Work 1ch, 18dc into ring, join with a ss into first dc.

2nd round: 1ch, 1dc into first dc, *5ch, miss 1dc, 1dc into next dc, rep from * to end omitting 1dc at end of last rep, ss into first dc. Fasten off.

3rd Flower: (make 2)
With 5.00mm (UK 6) hook and D, make 6ch, join with a ss into first ch to form a ring.

1st round: Work 1ch, 18dc into ring, join with a ss into first dc.

2nd round: 1ch, 1dc into first dc, *5ch, 1dc into next dc, rep from * to end omitting 1dc at end of last rep, ss into first dc. Fasten off.

 ## Making up

Cut fabric in half to make two 23 x 25cm (9 x10in) pieces. Turn 1cm (⅜in) hem to WS around all edges of both pieces and sew in place to neaten. With WS together and aligning top edge of lining just below scalloped top edge of Cosy, attach a fabric lining to both Cosy pieces with running stitch.

With RS of Cosy facing, join one side seam for spout, leaving a gap about 10cm (4in) wide and 3cm (1¼in) up from lower edge (adjust opening to fit teapot). Join other side seam for about 10cm (4in) from top edge, then leave rest of seam open (for handle). With 5.00mm (UK 6) hook, join A to lower open edge of handle seam, make 6ch, ss to same seam edge about 1cm (½in) above to form a button loop. Attach a button to opposite side of handle seam to correspond with button loop.

Starting at centre of row, thread drawstring in and out of lace holes along second row from top of cosy. At each end of drawstring, sew one 1st, 2nd or 3rd flower to each of 3 chain lengths and use it to gather up top of cosy, tying in a bow.

Clutch bag with flowers

Create a funky clutch bag and then decorate
it with brightly coloured flowers.

Neat and elegantly simple with integral handles, this little clutch bag is worked is double crochet with brightly coloured 'flowers' stitched on afterwards.

GETTING STARTED

★ *Bag is worked in a basic fabric with clear instructions for making handle slits.*

Size:
Bag is 27cm (10½in) wide x 20cm (8in) high

How much yarn:
3 x 50g (1¾oz) balls of Debbie Bliss Cashmerino DK in colour A – Purple (shade 36)
1 ball in each of two contrast colours: colour B – Bright Pink (shade 22) and colour C – Green (shade 11)

Hook:
4.00mm (UK 8) crochet hook

Additional items:
35 x 70cm (13¾ x 27½in) rectangle of lining fabric
Heavyweight, iron-on interfacing
Sewing needle and thread

Tension:
16 dc and 20 rows measure 10cm (4in) square on 4.00mm (UK 8) hook
IT IS ESSENTIAL TO WORK TO THE STATED TENSION TO ACHIEVE SUCCESS

What you have to do:
Work back, front and gusset of bag in double crochet. Make slits in crochet fabric for handles using graduated stitches and chain loop. Neaten top edge and around handle slits with slip stitch edging. Make appliqué flowers in rounds to decorate bag. Sew simple fabric lining to neaten inside of bag.

The Yarn
Debbie Bliss Cashmerino DK (approx. 110m/120 yards per 50g/1¾oz ball) contains 55% merino wool, 33% microfibre and 12% cashmere. It makes a soft, luxurious fabric that can be machine-washed at a low temperature. There are plenty of fabulous shades to choose from.

Instructions

BACK:

With 4.00mm (UK 8) hook and A, make 43ch loosely.

Foundation row: (RS) 1dc into 2nd ch from hook, 1dc into each ch to end, turn. 42 sts.

Next row: 1ch, 1dc into first dc, 1dc into each dc to end, turn.

Rep last row 26 times more.

Form handle:

Next row: (RS) 1ch, 1dc into each of next 9dc, 1htr into next dc, 1tr into next dc, 1dtr into next dc, 1tr tr into next dc, 16ch, miss 16 dc, 1tr tr into next dc, 1dtr into next dc, 1tr into next dc, 1htr into next dc, 1dc into each of next 9dc, turn.

Next row: 1ch, work 1dc into each st to end, turn. 42 sts.

Work 5 more rows in dc. Fasten off.

FRONT:

Work as given for Back, but do not fasten off at end.

Gusset:

With RS facing, work 1dc into each row down one side edge of front, 39dc along lower edge and 1dc into each row up other side edge, turn. 109 sts.

Work 10 rows in dc. Fasten off.

LARGE PINK FLOWER:

With 4.00mm (UK 8) hook and B, make 8ch, join with a ss into first ch to form a ring.

1st round: 2ch (counts as first htr), work 14htr into ring, join with a ss into 2nd of 2ch. 15 sts.

2nd round: *6ch, miss 2 sts, ss into next st, rep from * to end. 5 loops.

3rd round: Into each loop, work (1dc, 2htr, 2tr, 2htr and 1dc), join with a ss into first dc. Fasten off.

LARGE GREEN FLOWER:

With 4.00mm (UK 8) hook and C, make 8ch, join with a ss into first ch to form a ring.

1st round: 2ch (counts as first htr), work 14htr into ring, join with a ss into 2nd of 2ch. 15 sts.

2nd round: *6ch, miss 2 sts, ss into next st, rep from to end. 5 loops.

3rd round: Into each loop, work (1dc, 2htr, 2tr, 2htr and 1dc), join with a ss into first dc. Fasten off.

4th round: Rejoin yarn in space between 2htr at top of first petal, * working into front loops only, ss in each of next 4 sts, 6ch, ss between 2htr at top of next petal, rep from * 4 times more, join with a ss into first ss. 5 loops.

5th round: Working into back loops only, ss in each of next 4 sts, work (1dc, 2htr, 2tr, 2htr, 1dc) into each loop, join with a ss into first ss. Fasten off.

SMALL GREEN FLOWER:

With 4.00mm (UK 8) hook and C, make 3ch, join with a ss into first ch to form a ring.

1st round: Work 10dc into ring, join with a ss into first dc.

2nd round: *3ch, miss 1 st, ss into next st, rep from * to end. 5 loops.

3rd round: Into each loop, work (1dc, 2htr and 1dc), join with a ss into first dc. Fasten off.

SMALL PINK FLOWER:

With 4.00mm (UK 8) hook and B, make 3ch, join with a ss into first ch to form a ring.

1st round: Work 10dc into ring, join with a ss into first dc.

2nd round: *4ch, miss 1 st, ss into next st, rep from * to end. 5 loops.

3rd round: Into each loop, work (1dc, 3htr and 1dc), join with a ss into first dc.
Fasten off.

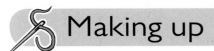 ## Making up

With WS facing, join edges of gusset to sides and lower edge of Back with a ss seam. Turn bag RS out.

Edging:

With 4.00mm (UK 8) hook, B and RS of work facing, work 1ss around stem of each st around top edge of bag, ss into first ss. Fasten off.

With B, edge handle openings with a round of ss worked around stem of dc along lower edge and into ch at top with 3ss in tr tr at each side, ss into first ss. Fasten off.

Sew flowers to front of bag in positions as shown.

Cut two 30 x 23cm (12 x 9in) rectangles of lining fabric and a strip 8.5 x 70cm (3⅜ x 27½in) Cut two rectangles of interfacing to fit top half of each fabric rectangle to strengthen handles and a strip to fit centre section of

narrow strip for bag base. Iron in place on WS of fabric, following the manufacturer's instructions.

Taking 1.5cm (⅝in) seam allowance, make up lining in same way as bag. Insert lining into bag. Fold over top edge of lining to WS so that it sits just below top of bag and slip stitch in position around top edge. Mark position of handle holes. Cut a central slit in lining, then cut diagonally into corners. Neaten handles by folding under lining to WS and slip stitching in place around edge of each handle hole.

Cupcake pincushions

Keep your pins in place with these cute pincushions.

Good enough to eat, these 'sweet' cupcakes made in simple stitches and embellished with flowers make ideal pincushions.

GETTING STARTED

 Cupcakes are easy to construct but attention to detail is required when adding decorations.

Size:
Finished cupcake measures 5.5cm (2¼in) in diameter across base x 9cm (3½in) tall

How much yarn:
1 x 50g (1¾oz) ball of Anchor Style Creativa Fino in each of seven colours: A – Grape (shade 01329); B – Orange (shade 01338); C – Light Pink (shade 01317); D – Gold (shade 01337); E – Yellow (shade 01311); F – Green (shade 01330); G – Pink (shade 01320)

Hook:
2.50mm (UK 12) crochet hook

Additional items:
Seed beads in yellow and peach
Gold thread and tapestry needle
Polyester toy filling

Tension:
Base of cupcake measures 5.5cm (2¼in) in diameter after 3rd round on 2.50mm (UK 12) hook
IT IS ESSENTIAL TO WORK TO THE STATED TENSION TO ACHIEVE SUCCESS

What you have to do:
Make cupcake cases and tops in rounds of simple stitches, shaping as directed. Stuff cases and tops with toy filling and sew together. Make flower decorations and sew to top of cupcakes. Embroider embellishments or sew on beads.

The Yarn
Anchor Style Creativa Fino (approx. 125m/136 yards per 50g/1¾oz ball) is a fine yarn in 100% mercerized cotton that is ideal for craft projects. It produces a smooth fabric with a slight sheen and there is a wide range of exciting colours to choose from.

Instructions

Abbreviations:

ch = chain(s)

cm = centimetre(s)

cont = continue

dc = double crochet

dtr = double treble

foll = follow(ing)(s)

htr = half treble

RS = right side

ss = slip stitch

st(s) = stitch(es)

tr = treble

WS = wrong side

CUPCAKE CASE: (make 1 each in A and B)

With 2.50mm (UK 12) hook make a magic circle (see Note on page 54).

1st round: 3ch (counts as first tr), work 14tr into ring, join with a ss into 3rd of 3ch and tighten end of yarn to close hole. 15 sts.

2nd round: 3ch, 2tr into each st, 1tr into same place as ss at end of last round, join with a ss into 3rd of 3ch. 30 sts.

3rd round: 3ch, (2tr into next st, 1tr into

foll st) to last st, 2tr into last st, join with a ss into 3rd of 3ch. 45 sts.

4th round: 1ch (does not count as a st), ss into back loop only of each st to end.

5th–10th rounds: 2ch (counts as first htr), 1htr into each st to end, join with a ss into 2nd of 2ch. 45 sts.

11th round: 2ch, 1htr into st at base of ch, 1htr into each of foll 8 sts, (2htr into next st, 1htr into each of foll 8 sts) 4 times, join with a ss into 2nd of 2ch. 50 sts.

12th round: 2ch, 1htr into each st to end, join with a ss into 2nd of 2ch. Fasten off.

For case in A, use same colour to embroider long running sts on side of case, spacing each long st about 2 sts apart. Start each st in 5th round and end in 11th round.

CUPCAKE TOP:

(make 1 in C to go with case in A and 1 in D to go with case in B)

Work as given for Cupcake case to completion of 1st round.

2nd round: 2ch, 2htr into each st, 1htr

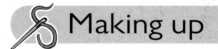

MARIGOLD FLOWER:

With 2.50mm (UK 12) hook and E, make a magic circle (see Note on page 54).

1st round: 1ch, work 5dc into ring and tighten end of yarn to close hole. 5 sts. Work in continuous rounds as foll:

2nd round: 2dc into each st to end. 10 sts.

3rd round: (2ch, 1tr and 1dtr into next st, 2ch, ss into foll st) 5 times. Fasten off leaving a long end.

Thread yarn end into needle and take through to RS of centre of flower and work a French knot, take yarn to WS again and fasten off leaving a long end.

Leaf: (make 2)

With 2.50mm (UK 12) hook and F, make 7ch.

1st round: Ss into 2nd ch from hook, 1dc into each of next 2ch, 1htr into foll ch, 1tr into next ch, 1htr into last ch, 1ch, then cont working into loops along other side of foundation ch: 1htr into next ch, 1tr into foll ch, 1htr into next ch, 1dc into each of foll 2ch, ss into next ch. Fasten off leaving a long tail.

into same place as ss at end of last round, join with a ss into 2nd of 2ch. 30 sts.

3rd round: 2ch, (2htr into next st, 1htr into foll st) to last st, 2htr into last st, join with a ss into 2nd of 2ch. 45 sts.

4th round: 2ch, 1htr into each htr to end, join with a ss into 2nd of 2ch. 45 sts.

5th round: 2ch, 1htr into st at base of ch, 1htr into each of foll 8 sts, (2htr into next st, 1htr into each of foll 8 sts) 4 times, join with a ss into 2nd of 2ch. 50 sts.

6th and 7th rounds: As 4th. 50 sts.

8th round: 2ch, 1htr into st at base of ch, 1htr into each of foll 9 sts, (2htr into next st, 1htr into each of foll 9 sts) 4 times, join with a ss into 2nd of 2ch. 55 sts.

9th round: (Miss next st, 5tr into foll st, miss next st, ss into each of foll 2 sts) to end. Fasten off leaving a long end.

CARNATION FLOWER:

With 2.50mm (UK 12) hook and G, make 5ch, join with a ss into first ch to form a circle.

1st round: (8ch, ss into circle) 12 times. Fasten off leaving a long tail.

Weave yarn tail through ring, tighten to draw petals upwards, secure with a back stitch and fasten off leaving a long tail.

Sepals:

With 2.50mm (UK 12) hook and F, make a magic circle (see Note on page 54).

1st round: 1ch, work 10dc into ring, join with a ss into first dc and tighten end of yarn to close hole.

2nd round: (3ch, 1tr and 1dtr into next st, 3ch, ss into foll st) 5 times. Fasten off leaving a long tail.

Making up

Stuff cupcake case firmly with toy filling and lightly stuff underside of cake top. Position cake top on to case and sew together, leaving a small gap. Finish stuffing cake top before firmly closing hole.

Carnation cupcake:

Sew carnation on to middle of sepals, then sew flower to cake top. Using 2 strands of G, sew short running sts to represent 'sprinkles' over surface of cake top.

Marigold cupcake:

Sew marigold on to top of cake, with one leaf at each side of flower. Sew seed beads onto cake top using gold thread.

Daisy-edged bolero

Pastel-coloured flowers make a pretty edging for this very wearable bolero.

Make this stylish boxy bolero with three-quarter length sleeves in a soft cotton yarn and filet mesh pattern, then embellish it with contrast-coloured flowers worked directly on to the fabric.

GETTING STARTED

 Mesh pattern for bolero is straight-forward but there is a lot of shaping and working flowers requires practice.

Size:

To fit bust: 81–86[91–96]cm (32–34[36–38]in)
Actual size: 85[95]cm (33½[37½]in)
Length: 37[41]cm (14½[16]in)
Sleeve seam: 36[38]cm (14[15]in)
Note: Figures in square brackets [ ] refer to larger size; where there is only one set of figures, it applies to both sizes

How much yarn:

5[7] x 50g (1¾oz) balls of DMC Natura in colour A – Sable (shade 3)
1 ball in each of three contrast colours: B – Topaze (shade 19); C – Blue Paradise (shade 24) and D – Spring Rose (shade 7)

Hooks:

2.50mm (UK 12) crochet hook
3.00mm (UK 11) crochet hook

Tension:

24 sts and 10 rows measure 10cm (4in) square over patt on 3.00mm (UK 11) hook
IT IS ESSENTIAL TO WORK TO THE STATED TENSION TO ACHIEVE SUCCESS

What you have to do:

Work bolero in main colour and alternate mesh pattern, shaping armholes, neck and sleeves as directed. Neaten front, neck, hem and cuff edges with rounds of double crochet and picot edging. Use contrast colours to make flowers as required, working each flower around a hole in mesh pattern.

The Yarn

DMC Natura Just Cotton (approx. 155m/169 yards per 50g/1¾oz ball) contains 100% combed cotton threads with a matt finish. Soft and versatile, it produces a machine-washable fabric, pleasant to wear. There is a good colour range.

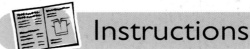 Instructions

BACK:

With 3.00mm (UK 11) hook and A, make 104[116]ch.

Foundation row: (RS) 1tr in 4th ch from hook, *2ch, miss next 2ch, 1tr in each of foll 4ch, rep from * to last 4ch, 2ch, miss next 2ch, 1tr in each of last 2ch, turn. 102[114] sts.

Cont in alt mesh patt as foll:

1st row: 3ch (counts as first tr), miss st at base of ch, *1tr in next tr, 2tr in 2ch sp, 1tr in next tr, 2ch, miss foll 2tr; rep from * to last 5 sts, 1tr in next tr, 2tr in 2ch sp, 1tr in next tr, 1tr in 3rd of 3ch, turn.

2nd row: 3ch, miss st at base of ch, 1tr in next tr, *2ch, miss next 2tr, 1tr in next tr, 2tr in 2ch sp, 1tr in next tr, rep from * to last 4 sts, 2ch, miss next 2tr, 1tr in next tr, 1tr in 3rd of 3ch, turn. Rep last 2 rows 6[7] more times, then work 1st row again. 16[18] rows.

Shape armholes:

1st dec row: (RS) Ss in each of first 7 sts, 3ch, miss st at base of ch, 1tr in next tr, miss foll 2tr, 1tr in next tr, patt to last 10 sts, miss next 2tr, 1tr in foll tr, 1tr in first of 2ch, turn leaving 6 sts unworked. 86[98] sts.

2nd dec row: 3ch, miss st at base of ch, tr2tog over next 2tr, patt to last 3 sts, tr2tog over next 2 sts, 1tr in 3rd of 3ch, turn. 1 st dec at each end of row.

Abbreviations:

alt = alternate
beg = beginning
ch = chain(s)
cm = centimetre(s)
cont = continue
dc = double crochet
dc2tog = (insert hook in next st, yrh and draw a loop through) twice, yrh and draw through all 3 loops on hook
dec = decrease(d)
foll = follow(ing)(s)
patt = pattern
rep = repeat
RS = right side
ss = slip stitch
st(s) = stitch(es)
tr = treble
tr2tog = (yrh, insert hook as directed, yrh and draw through a loop, yrh and draw through first 2 loops on hook) twice, yrh and draw through all 3 loops on hook
WS = wrong side
yrh = yarn round hook

3rd dec row: 3ch, miss st at base of ch, tr2tog over next st and foll ch sp, 1tr in next tr, patt to last ch sp, tr2tog over ch sp and foll st, 1tr in 3rd of 3ch, turn. 2 sts dec at each end of row.

4th dec row: 3ch, miss st at base of ch and next st, patt to last 2 sts, miss next st, 1tr in 3rd of 3ch, turn. 78[90] sts. Work a further 13[15] rows in patt, ending with a RS row.

Shape back neck:

Next row: Patt 17[23] sts, miss next 2tr, 1tr in foll tr, turn and complete this side of neck first. 18[24] sts.
Patt 1 row. 19[21] rows from beg of armholes. Fasten off. With WS of work facing, miss 38 sts at centre neck, rejoin yarn in next tr, 3ch, miss st at base of ch and next 2tr, 1tr in next tr, patt to end, turn. 18[24] sts.
Patt 1 row. Fasten off.

LEFT FRONT:

With 3.00mm (UK 11) hook and A, make 50[56]ch. Work foundation row as given for Back. 48[54] sts. Work 15[17] rows in patt as given for Back, ending with a WS row.**

Shape armhole:

1st dec row: (RS) Ss in each of first 7 sts, 3ch, miss st at base of ch, 1tr in next tr, miss foll 2tr, 1tr in next tr, patt to end, turn. 40[46] sts.

2nd dec row: Patt to last 3 sts, tr2tog over next 2 sts, 1tr in 3rd of 3ch, turn.

3rd dec row: 3ch, miss st at base of ch, tr2tog over next st and foll ch sp, 1tr in next tr, patt to end, turn.

4th dec row: Patt to last 2 sts, miss next st, 1tr in 3rd of 3ch, turn. 36[42] sts. Keeping patt correct, work 5[7] more rows, ending with a RS row. 9[11] rows from beg of armhole.

Shape neck:

1st neck row: Ss in each of first 10 sts, 3ch, miss st at base of ch, 1tr in next tr, miss foll 2tr, 1tr in next tr, patt to end, turn. 25[31] sts.

2nd neck row: Patt to last 3 sts, tr2tog over next 2 sts, 1tr in 3rd of 3ch, turn. 24[30] sts.

3rd neck row: 3ch, miss st at base of ch, tr2tog over next st and foll ch sp, 1tr in next tr, patt to end, turn. 22[28] sts.

4th neck row: Patt to last 2 sts, miss next st, 1tr in 3rd of 3ch, turn. 21[27] sts.

5th neck row: 3ch, miss st at base of ch, 1tr in next tr, miss foll 2tr, 1tr in next tr, patt to end, turn. 19[25] sts.

6th neck row: As 2nd neck row. 18[24] sts. Work 4 more rows without shaping. 19[21] rows from beg of armhole. Fasten off.

RIGHT FRONT:

Work as given for Left front to **.

Shape armhole:

1st dec row: Patt to last 10 sts, miss next 2tr, 1tr in foll tr, 1tr in first of 2ch, turn leaving 6 sts unworked. 40[46] sts.

2nd dec row: 3ch, miss st at base of ch, tr2tog over next 2tr, patt to end, turn.

3rd dec row: Patt to last ch sp, tr2tog over ch sp and foll tr, 1tr in 3rd of 3ch, turn.

4th dec row: 3ch, miss st at base of ch and foll st, patt to end, turn. 36[42] sts. Keeping patt correct, work 5[7] more rows, ending with a RS row. 9[11] rows from beg of armhole.

Shape neck:

1st neck row: Patt to last 13 sts, miss next 2tr, 1tr in foll tr, 1tr in next ch sp, turn leaving 9 sts unworked. 25[31] sts.

2nd neck row: 3ch, miss st at base of ch, tr2tog over next 2 sts, patt to end, turn. 24[30] sts.

3rd neck row: Patt to last ch sp, tr2tog over ch sp and foll tr, 1tr in 3rd of 3ch, turn. 22[28] sts.

4th neck row: 3ch, miss st at base of ch and foll st, patt to end, turn. 21[27] sts.

5th neck row: Patt to last 4 sts, miss next 2tr, 1tr in foll tr, 1tr in 3rd of 3ch, turn. 19[25] sts.

6th neck row: As 2nd neck row. 18[24] sts.

Work 4 more rows without shaping. 19[21] rows from beg of armhole. Fasten off.

SLEEVES: (make 2)

With 3.00mm (UK 11) hook and A, make 68[74]ch. Work foundation row as given for Back. 66[72] sts. Work 5 rows in patt as given for Back, ending with a WS row.

Shape sleeve:

7th row: 3ch, miss st at base of ch, 2tr in next tr, patt to last 2 sts, 2tr in next tr, 1tr in 3rd of 3ch, turn. 68[74] sts. Working new sts as 1ch on WS rows and 1tr on RS row, patt 3 rows.

11th row: 3ch, miss st at base of ch, 2tr in 1ch sp, patt to last 1ch sp, 2tr in 1ch sp, 1tr in 3rd of 3ch, turn. 70[76] sts. Working new sts as another ch on WS rows and another tr on RS row, patt 3 rows.

15th row: 3ch, miss st at base of ch, 3tr in 2ch sp, patt to last 2ch sp, 3tr in 2ch sp, 1tr in 3rd of 3ch, turn. 72[78] sts. Patt 3 rows.

19th row: 4ch, miss st at base of ch, patt to last st, 1ch, 1tr in 3rd of 3ch, turn. 74[80] sts. Working new sts as 1tr in 1ch sp on WS rows and 1ch on RS row, patt 3 rows.

23rd row: 5ch, miss st at base of ch and next tr, 1tr in next tr, patt to last 2 sts, 2ch, miss next tr, 1tr in 3rd of 3ch, turn. 76[82] sts. Working new sts as another tr on WS rows and another ch on RS row, patt 3 rows.

27th row: 3ch, 1tr in st at base of ch, patt to last st, 2tr in 3rd of 3ch, turn. 78[84] sts. Patt 7[9] rows, ending with a WS row. 34[36] rows in all.

Shape top:

Work 1st–4th dec rows as given for Back armholes. 54[60] sts.

5th dec row: 3ch, miss st at base of ch, 1tr in next tr, miss foll 2tr, patt to last 4 sts, miss next 2tr, 1tr in foll tr, 1tr in 3rd of 3ch, turn.

6th–8th dec rows: Work 2nd–4th dec rows as given for Back armholes. 42[48] sts.

9th dec row: As 5th dec row.

1st size only:
Work 2nd and 3rd dec rows once more. 32 sts. Fasten off.

2nd size only:
Work 2nd–4th dec rows once more, then 5th dec row again. 32 sts. Fasten off.

Making up

Press according to directions on ball band. Join shoulder seams. Sew in sleeves, then join side and sleeve seams.

Front, hem and neck edging:

With 2.50mm (UK 12) hook and RS of work facing, join A at base of one side seam, 1ch (counts as first dc), 1dc in base of each tr and 2dc in each 2ch sp to lower front corner, 3dc in same place, 2dc in each row-end to front neck corner, 3dc in same place, 1dc in each tr, 2dc in each ch sp and 2dc in each row-end around neck edge to front neck corner, cont in this way all round, join with a ss in first ch.

2nd round: 1ch, 1dc in each dc all round, working 3dc in same place at each outward corner and dc2tog at front and back neck inner corners, join with a ss in first ch.

3rd round: 1ch, *3ch, 1dc in 3rd ch from hook, miss next dc, 1dc in foll dc, rep from * all round, ending 3ch, 1dc in 3rd ch from hook, miss next dc, join with a ss in first ch. Fasten off.

Cuffs:

With 2.50mm (UK 12) hook and RS of work facing, join A at base of sleeve seam, 1ch, 1dc in base of each tr and 2dc in each ch sp all round, join with a ss in first ch.

2nd round: 1ch, 1dc in each dc, join with a ss in first ch.

3rd round: Work as given for 3rd round of Front, hem and neck edging. Fasten off.

Add flowers:

You can add as many flowers as required around cuffs, front, hem and neck edges using colours B, C and D. Each flower is worked around a mesh hole. To plan arrangement of flowers, cut 10cm (4in) lengths of yarn in contrast colours and use to mark holes required.

Flower:

With 3.00mm (UK 11) hook and RS of work facing, leave a 10cm (4in) tail and join yarn to top of first of 2 empty tr at lower edge of a hole. Work around hole, enclosing tail of yarn as foll:

1st round: 1ch, 1dc in next tr, 1dc in corner, 2dc around stem of next tr at left edge, 1dc in corner, 1dc in base of each of 2tr at top of hole, 1dc in corner, 2dc around tr at right of hole, 1dc in corner, join with a ss in first ch. 12 sts.

2nd round: 4ch, (3tr in next dc, 2ch, 1dc in foll dc, 2ch) 5 times, 3tr in last dc, 2ch, join with a ss in first of 4ch. Fasten off.

Pull gently on enclosed starting tail to tighten centre of flower to a neat hole.

Flower-trimmed clutch bag

A clever design makes this striking purse truly unique.

This pretty purse is worked in a filet mesh fabric, trimmed with small rose motifs that are sewn onto surface crochet 'stems'. It is lined with matching stiffened fabric.

The Yarn

DMC Petra No. 3 (approx. 280m/305 yards per 100g/ 3½oz ball) is a 100% cotton mercerized thread that is perfect for craft items since it produces a soft and supple fabric. It is available in a wide range of both traditional pastel and strong colours.

GETTING STARTED

 Filet mesh fabric is easy to make but a good finish relies on attention to detail.

Size:
Finished purse measures 20cm (8in) wide x 14cm (5½in) high

How much yarn:
1 x 100g (3½oz) ball of DMC Petra No.3 in each of three colours: A – Turquoise (shade 53845); B – Bright Pink (shade 53805); C – Green (shade 5907)

Hook:
2.50mm (UK 12) crochet hook

Additional items:
45 x 45cm (18 x18in) piece of lining fabric
Sewing needle and matching thread
20 x 39cm (8 x 15½in) piece of iron-on stiffener
Magnetic clasp

Tension:
30 sts (10 ch sps) and 12 rows measure 10cm (4in) square over mesh patt on 2.50mm (UK 12) hook
IT IS ESSENTIAL TO WORK TO THE STATED TENSION TO ACHIEVE SUCCESS

What you have to do:
Make purse in filet mesh pattern, shaping point as directed. Work surface crochet lines on mesh for 'stems'. Make rose and leaf motifs and sew onto stems. Sew lining with added stiffening.

Instructions

Abbreviations:

beg = beginning
ch = chain(s)
cm = centimetre(s)
cont = continue
dc = double crochet
dec = decreased
foll = following
htr = half treble
patt = pattern
rep = repeat
RS = right side
sp(s) = space(s)
ss = slip stitch
st(s) = stitch(es)
tr = treble
WS = wrong side

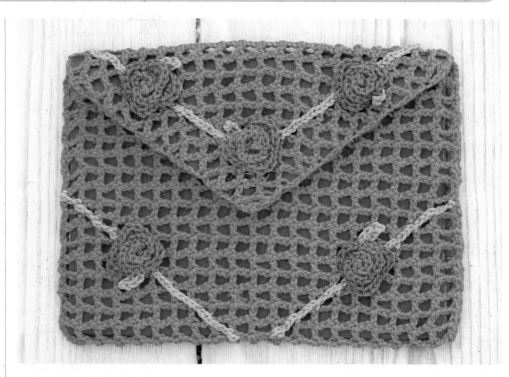

PURSE:

With 2.50mm (UK 12) hook and A, make 65ch.

Foundation row: (RS) 1tr into 8th ch from hook, *2ch, miss next 2ch, 1tr into next ch, rep from * to end, turn. 20 ch sps.

Next row: 5ch (counts as first tr and 2ch), miss first ch sp, 1tr into next tr, *2ch, 1tr into next tr, rep from * to end, working last tr into 5th of 7ch, turn.

Patt row: 5ch, miss first ch sp, 1tr into next tr, *2ch, 1tr into next tr, rep from * to end, working last tr into 3rd of 5ch, turn. Rep patt row 5 times more. Mark each end of last row (first pair of markers) to show joining points for surface crochet 'stems'.

Patt a further 9 rows. Mark each end of last row (2nd pair of markers) to show ending row for surface crochet stems and also fold line for lower edge of purse.

Patt 17 more rows. Mark each end of last row (3rd pair of markers) to show ending row for surface crochet stems to be worked on flap. Patt 2 more rows.

Shape point:

Next row: 3ch (counts as first tr), miss first ch sp, 1tr into next tr, *2ch, 1tr into next tr, rep from * to last ch sp, 1tr into 3rd of 5ch, turn. 18 ch sps.

Next row: 3ch, miss first ch sp, 1tr into next tr, patt to last ch sp, 1tr into 3rd of 3ch, turn. 1 sp dec at each end of row. Rep last row 7 times more. 2 ch sps.

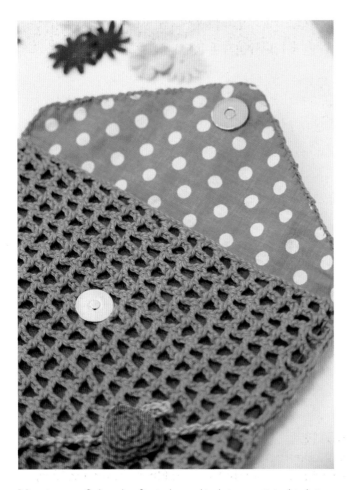

Next row: 3ch, miss first ch sp, 1tr into next tr, 1tr into 3rd of 3ch. Fasten off.

Surface crochet stems:

Left diagonal: With 2.50mm (UK 12) hook and RS of purse facing, join C to first marker at right-hand edge of purse. Holding yarn on WS of purse work 1ss in top of marked tr, insert hook in first ch sp in row above marker, 3ch, 1ss in top of 2nd tr from edge in same row, insert hook in 2nd ch sp in row above, 3ch, 1ss in top of 3rd tr from edge in same row, insert hook in 3rd ch sp in row above, 3ch, 1ss in top of 4th tr from edge in same row. Moving up one row, and one sp/one tr to the left each time, cont in this way, ending 1ss in top of tr on row with 2nd pair of markers. Fasten off.

Right diagonal: Joining C to first marker at left-hand edge, work to match left diagonal, moving up one row, and one sp/one tr to the right each time.

Turn work upside down. With RS facing, join C to top of centre tr on 4th row from point, 1ss in same place as join, now work left diagonal, ending with 1ss in top of tr on row with 3rd pair of markers. Fasten off. Rejoin C to centre tr on 4th row from point and work right diagonal to match left.

ROSE: (make 5)

With 2.50mm (UK 12) hook and B, make 25ch.

1st row: 2dc into 2nd ch from hook, 2dc into each of next 2ch, ss into next ch, 2dc into each of foll 3ch, ss into next st, 2dc into foll ch, 2htr into next ch, 2dc into foll ch, ss into next ch, *2htr into foll ch, 2tr into next ch, 2htr into foll ch, ss into next ch, rep from * to end. Fasten off. Coil up strip of petals, with smallest in centre, and sew together at base as you go along.

LEAF: (make 5)

With 2.50mm (UK 12) hook and C, make 5ch.

1st row: Ss into 2nd ch from hook, 1dc into each of next 2ch, ss into last ch. Fasten off.

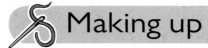

Making up

Sew a leaf behind each rose, then sew roses to surface crochet stems in positions as shown in photograph.

Lining:

Using crochet fabric as a template, cut two pieces of lining fabric, allowing 1cm (⅜in) extra on all sides. Also cut a piece of iron-on stiffener to same size as purse. Following manufacturer's directions, iron stiffener on to WS of one lining piece. With RS facing and taking a 1cm (⅜in) seam allowance, sew around all sides of lining fabric pieces, leaving a small gap for turning through. Turn RS out, neatly slip stitch opening closed and press.

With WS facing, fold up lower edge of purse at 2nd pair of markers and, using a sewing needle and thread, join side seams. Remove all markers. Repeat with lining. Attach magnetic clasp to lining fabric point and to corresponding position on front of crochet purse, following manufacturer's instructions.

Place lining inside purse and slip stitch lining to purse along front top edge and all around point.

Index

B

bags
  clutch bag with flowers 112
  felted bag with flower motifs 48
  flower corsage tote bag 32
  flower-sprinkled bag 84
  flower-trimmed clutch bag 124
belt, hippy 16
boleros
  bolero with flower motifs 56
  daisy-edged bolero 120
bracelets 28

C

chrysanthemum napkin ring 44
corsages, mini 20
cupcake pincushions 116
cushions
  folk-art cushion 12
  rose cushion 76

D

daffodil napkin ring 44
daisy napkin ring 44

F

flowers
  daffodil 46
  daisy 46, 91

carnation 119
chrysanthemum 47
fluted flowers 63
marigold 119
rose 45, 79
spiral flower 62

G

garden kneeler 88
gloves, flower-trimmed mesh 80

H

hair accessories
  beads and flowers hair clip 92
  floral hairband 64
  head cuff, flower 8
hats
  flower band hat 104
  Trilby hatbands 52
head cuff, flower 8
hippy belt 16

J

jacket, flower-edged 40

M

mats, funky flowers 68
mini corsages 20

N

napkin rings, floral 44

P

pincushions, cupcake 116
purse, heart-shaped 96

R

rose napkin ring 44

S

scarves
  embossed scarf 60
  floral medallion scarf 24
  flower scarf 36
  Spring fever scarf 100

T

tea cosy, funky 108

V

vest, floral appliqué 72

Acknowledgements

Managing Editor: Clare Churly
Editors: Lesley Malkin and Eleanor van Zandt
Senior Art Editor: Juliette Norsworthy
Designer: Janis Utton
Production Controller: Allison Gonsalves